UNDERSTANDING

ETERNAL SECURITY

BY

CHARLES F. STANLEY

THOMAS NELSON
Since 1798

Understanding Eternal Security

Charles F. Stanley

Copyright © 1998, 2008 by Charles F. Stanley

Published in Nashville, Tennessee, by Thomas Nelson, Inc.

G B

Editing, layout, and design by Gregory C. Benoit Publishing, Old Mystic, CT

The Bible version used in this publication is THE NEW KING JAMES VERSION. Copyright © 1979, 1980, 1982, Thomas Nelson, Inc., Publishers.

ISBN 978-1-4185-2814-0

Printed in the United States of America

08 09 10 11 12 RRD 5 4 3 2

Contents

Contents

INTRODUCTION

God's Perspective on Eternal Security

Each of us has a unique perspective on life. We have a distinct way of looking at things, judging things, and holding things in our memories. Our perspective is something that we have learned, and it is something that changes as we relearn or learn more about life. In my years of ministry, I have found that a wrong perspective is very common when it comes to personal salvation. Many have misconceptions about how they became born again—they err in their understanding about the basis for their salvation. Consequently, it is very easy for them to misunderstand how they might lose their salvation. They do not understand why God forgives, what it means to be saved, or how to live within the fullness of their salvation.

To gain the right perspective on eternal security, we must go to God's Word and stay there. The Bible is God's foremost communication to us on this topic. It is the reference to which we must return continually if we are to truly understand what has happened to us spiritually in a born-again experience, and to understand fully what that experience means for all eternity.

As you work your way through this study, keep your Bible at your side. As you study each passage, make notes in the margins of your Bible. Read the passage from Scripture for yourself. It is far more important that you write God's insights into your Bible than to write them in this booklet, although places are provided for you to make notes.

This book can be used by you alone or by several people in a small-group study. At various times, you will be asked to relate to the material in one of these four ways:

1. *What new insights have you gained?* Make notes about the insights that you have. You may want to record them in your Bible or in a separate journal. As you reflect back over your insights, you are likely to see how God has moved in your life.

2. *Have you ever had a similar experience?* Each of us approaches the Bible from a unique background—our own particular set of relationships and experiences. Our experiences do not make the Bible true—the Word of God is truth regardless of our opinion about it. It is important, however, to share our experiences in order to see how God's truth can be applied to human lives.

3. *How do you feel about the material presented?* Emotional responses do not give validity to the Scriptures, nor should we trust our emotions as a gauge for our faith. In small-group Bible study, however, it is good for participants to express their emotions. The Holy Spirit often communicates with us through this unspoken language.

4. *In what way do you feel challenged to respond or to act?* God's Word may cause you to feel inspired or challenged to change something in your life. Take the challenge seriously and find ways of acting upon it. If God reveals to you a particular need that He wants *you* to address, take that as "marching orders" from God. God is expecting you to *do* something with the challenge that He has just given you.

Start and conclude your Bible study sessions in prayer. Ask God to give you spiritual eyes to see and spiritual ears to hear. As you conclude your study, ask the Lord to seal what you have learned so that you will never forget it. Ask Him to help you grow into the fullness of the stature of Christ Jesus.

Again, I caution you to keep the Bible at the center of your study. A genuine Bible study stays focused on God's Word and promotes a growing faith and a closer walk with the Holy Spirit in *each* person who participates.

You Can Know with Certainty

LEARNING: WHAT IS "ETERNAL SECURITY" ANYWAY?

GROWING: HOW CAN I KNOW FOR CERTAIN WHERE I WILL SPEND ETERNITY?

Every time that we offer a tape series on eternal security, the response is overwhelming. I am always amazed at the great number of people who are interested in this topic, and who apparently do not have the absolute assurance that they are saved. Many of these people are believers in Christ Jesus and have had a genuine salvation experience, yet they do not know with *certainty* that they will go to heaven when they die.

Essentially there are five categories of people in our world today:

1. Those who are unsaved and know that they are unsaved. They have no security regarding their eternal future.

2. Those who are unsaved but think that they are saved. They have a false security about eternity.

3. Those who are saved but are uncertain about whether they are saved. They are insecure.

4. Those who believe that they were saved but who are unsure about their salvation. They have a feeling of security in the here and now, but they are not "eternally" secure.

5. Those who are certain that they have been saved, are saved, and will be saved forever. They are the ones who truly are "eternally secure" in their salvation experience.

It is my great hope that by the time you complete this study, you will be among that last category of believers in Christ Jesus—knowing that you are saved forever by your personal acceptance of what Jesus did for you on the cross.

Falling from Grace

The opposite belief regarding eternal security is one generally called "falling from grace." According to this position, a person can "lose" his salvation through sin and wayward living after a salvation experience. I once argued this viewpoint very strongly.

What caused me to become a firm believer in the truth of eternal security? While I was in seminary working on a particular passage of the New Testament in a Greek course, I had one of those irrefutable "dawning of the truth" experiences in my life. I saw clearly that a person can have a *sure* understanding of *eternal* security and a destiny that is forever linked to that of Jesus Christ. I began to search the Scriptures in earnest, reading everything I could to compare the two approaches. I no longer was trying to prove my earlier position that a person might "fall from grace," and neither was I doubting the new insight that I had into the Scriptures. In effect, I was in a neutral position.

The more I studied *all* of the passages of the New Testament that deal with eternal security, sin, and grace, the more I saw that God provides eternal security for those who believe in Jesus Christ. Most Christians, I have found, do not truly study this topic—rather, they cling to whatever position they were taught as children. When we accept without genuine *understanding* the tenets of our faith, we can easily be led into error. I am not asking you to doubt all that you have learned about God, Jesus Christ, the Holy Spirit, or the Bible. Rather, I am asking you to *look for yourself* into the depths of the Scriptures on this topic and gain an understanding that is born of your own study.

A Baptist Doctrine?

Many people associate the topic of eternal security with a doctrinal position of "once saved, always saved." In turn, they associate this doctrine with Baptists, as well as several other denominations. The fact of the matter is, however, that eternal security is not a doctrinal issue—it is a matter of biblical truth. This Bible study is just that, a *Bible* study, not a doctrinal study.

I encourage you to fully investigate this topic before you draw a firm conclusion about eternal security. Be careful not to condemn before you investigate. As has been said by many through the ages, "Condemnation before investigation leads to error."

If you are not born again, I pray that this study will lead you to accept Jesus Christ as your Savior. If you are born again, then I trust that this study will lead you to place an even greater confidence in what Jesus Christ purchased for you with His blood. If you are doubting your salvation, or questioning your eternal destiny as a born-again believer, I trust that this study will settle your doubts once and for all. You can know with assurance that Jesus Christ is your Savior *forever*.

❧ Have you accepted Jesus Christ as your Lord and Savior? If not, what is holding you back?

Yes

❧ Have you experienced God's forgiveness in your life? Have you come to a full understanding and assurance about your heavenly home and eternal destiny?

No

❧ Which of the five groups listed above are you in? If you're *not* in group 5, why?

Group 5

❧ Today and Tomorrow ❧

TODAY: I UNDERSTAND THAT IT IS POSSIBLE TO KNOW FOR CERTAIN WHERE I WILL SPEND ETERNITY.

TOMORROW: I WILL SPEND TIME IN PRAYER AND BIBLE STUDY, ASKING GOD TO TEACH ME ABOUT ETERNAL SECURITY.

LESSON 2

The Nature of Your Salvation

❧ In This Lesson ❧

LEARNING: WHAT DOES IT MEAN TO BE "BORN AGAIN"?

GROWING: HOW CAN I HOPE TO SEE REAL CHANGE IN MY LIFE?

As we begin our study of eternal security, we must keep two definitions very clearly in mind:

> *Salvation:* Deliverance from eternal death, and possession of eternal life.

> *Eternal Security:* That work of God which guarantees that God's gift of salvation, once received, is possessed forever and can never be lost.

These two terms are vital to your hope and confidence as a Christian, as well as to your witness for Christ. Confusion about *how* you were saved leads to confusion about how a person might *remain* saved.

What It Means to Be "Saved"

To be saved from sin's consequences is *not* synonymous with:

❧ Dropping bad behaviors and adopting good ones in order to "get right with God"

❧ Joining a church

❧ Deciding to call yourself a Christian

❧ Going to the altar and saying that you are sorry for your sins

❧ Adding Christian disciplines such as prayer or Bible reading to your daily routine

All of these things are "works" of some kind. Salvation comes by *faith*. Salvation is the result of believing, not a by-product of doing.

Nicodemus was a very religious man in the time of Jesus. But Jesus told him that the good works which he had done did not make him born again spiritually.

❧ Read John 3:5–8, 14–18. What does it mean to be "born of water and the Spirit"? What does it mean to be "born of the flesh"?

womb and Spirit ↗

❧ What does it mean to "believe in" Jesus Christ? Do *you* believe in Jesus Christ?

persuaded to be true
committed to the truth
this belief is long
committed to the truth
of this particular belief

8

The Root Problem of a Sin Nature

Jesus made it very clear to Nicodemus that mankind has a sin problem. Furthermore, that sin problem means that mankind is "condemned already" (John 3:18). People *will* perish and be separated from God eternally if they do not face their sin problem and receive God's provision for it. Jesus spoke very clearly about this in Matthew 25:

෧ "Cast the unprofitable servant into the outer darkness. There will be weeping and gnashing of teeth" (v. 30).

෧ "He will also say to those on the left hand, 'Depart from Me, you cursed, into the everlasting fire prepared for the devil and his angel's'" (v. 41).

෧ "These will go away into everlasting punishment, but the righteous into eternal life" (v. 46).

"Sin" is going beyond the boundaries established by God. It is not only a behavioral problem, however—it is a "nature" problem, an identity or "state of being" problem. Man's sin nature is one of pride, greed, and total self-centeredness and self-will. Every person is born with this sin nature. Behavior is learned, but natural tendencies are not. A sin nature is inherent, and it is inherent regardless of the spiritual condition of our parents. It is part of our inheritance as fallen human beings, the descendants of Adam and Eve.

Now, a person might change his behavior as an act of the will, but he cannot change his basic sin nature, regardless of how much "willpower" is exerted. We are incapable of transforming our spirits or of altering the core of our spiritual being. We are born with a "sin condition" that only God can correct. The good news is that, while we were in this helpless, ungodly state, God sent His Son, Jesus, to die for us so that we do not have to be separated from God. We *can* be transformed and made new in spirit.

> For when we were still without strength, in due time Christ died for the ungodly.... But God demonstrates His own love toward us, in that while we were still sinners, Christ died for us.... For if when we were enemies we were reconciled to God through the death of His Son, much more, having been reconciled, we shall be saved by His life.

> —Romans 5:6, 8, 10

How does the death of Christ "demonstrate God's love toward us"?

he died for us even though we were sinners—

undeserving

Put verse 10 into your own words. How does the love of God bring us eternal security?

Re settled we are brought together

Books are brought → Kept safe from

Rescued from danger

God's Provision for Man's Sin Problem

God has a provision for man's sin problem—a provision born of His love. Every man and woman is the object of God's love, regardless of past deeds. It is wrong, however, to conclude that every person is "accepted" or has been made acceptable to God. God loves each person with an unfathomable love, but God's pure and holy nature cannot co-exist with sin. In order for man and God to be fully reconciled, the nature of man must be changed from a sin (wrong) nature to a righteous (right) nature. Only when this transformation has been made and a person has been "born again" is that person accepted by God.

Many people in our world today wrongly conclude that, because God loves everybody, He will save everybody. That is not what the Bible teaches. Jesus made it very clear that sin has consequences, including eternal consequences, but that God has made a provision for the sin nature of man to be changed. Man must act on that provision if he is to avoid the punishment reserved for those who enter eternity with an unchanged sin nature.

Believing and Receiving

Jesus told Nicodemus that receiving God's provision is a simple matter of believing. Jesus said, "Whoever believes in Him should not perish but have everlasting life" (John 3:16). Jesus also explained the basis on which Nicodemus must believe: "As Moses lifted up the serpent in the wilderness, even so must the Son of Man be lifted up" (John 3:14). "Lifted up" was a reference to Jesus being raised upon a cross.

🕮 Read Numbers 21:5–9, to which Jesus referred.

The only thing that the Israelites had to do was to *look* at the serpent to be saved from death. Jesus said that this same pattern would hold true for those who "looked" upon His death on the cross. All that a person needs to do today to be saved from sin is to look at Jesus on the cross, believing that He was and is forever God's sole provision for man's sin problem. A belief in Jesus as God's Son and as God's sacrifice for the sins of man is what saves a person. *Nothing less will do, but nothing more is required.*

What Does It Mean to "Believe"?

"Believing in Jesus" does not mean believing that He once lived on this earth, or that He was a good man or a fine religious teacher. Believing in Jesus means to place one's trust in Jesus as the only One who can bring forgiveness of sin. It means believing that Jesus was God's only begotten Son who paid the debt for *your* sin and who therefore qualifies to be *your* Savior. Believing in Jesus means believing that Jesus' death on the cross was:

Substitutionary: Jesus dies in *your* place, on account of *your* sin.

Atoning: Jesus' death makes it possible for you to be restored to God and accepted by Him.

Sacrificial: The shedding of His blood brought about a new relationship between you and God.

All who believe in the substitutionary, atoning, sacrificial death of Jesus are *saved*. That is what it means to be saved.

➤ Put into your own words the idea that Jesus' death was "substitutionary."

➤ If Jesus died for *your* sins, how does that affect your eternal security?

God's Promises and God's Provision

When we accept Christ as our Savior, we receive two promises: one related to *quantity* of life, the other to *quality* of life.

∞ An Everlasting Quantity of Life ∞

Jesus said to Nicodemus, "Whoever believes ... should not perish but have everlasting life" (John 3:16). In many versions of the Bible the word *should* in this verse is translated "will" or "shall." The intent of Jesus is that whoever believes will *undeniably* be given everlasting life by God. There are no qualifiers to this promise—no ifs, ands, or buts.

The promise of a heavenly home was also made by Jesus in John 14:1-4:

> Let not your heart be troubled; you believe in God, believe also in Me. In My Father's house are many mansions; if it were not so, I would have told you. I go to prepare a place for you. And if I go and prepare a place for you, I will come again and receive you to Myself; that where I am, there you may be also. And where I go you know, and the way you know.

❧ What does Jesus mean when He tells us not to let our hearts be troubled? What sort of "heart troubles" make us insecure about eternal security?

❧ According to this passage, how do we know that our "place" is absolutely secure?

∽ A New Quality of Life ∽

Jesus said that, upon believing in Him, a person is "birthed" by the Holy Spirit. Read again what Jesus said to Nicodemus: "That which is born of the Spirit is spirit" (John 3:6). When you accept Jesus as your Savior, the Spirit causes your spirit to be reborn or made new.

Note two very important things about this rebirth by the Spirit:

1. *The Spirit does the birthing.* You cannot make yourself be "born again." Your part is to look upon the Cross and believe in Jesus to receive God's forgiveness. God's part is to bring about the transformation of your spiritual nature.

2. *Once a person has received the Holy Spirit into his life, he will have a desire to love God, serve God, and walk in the ways of God.* The person who has been truly born anew will want to live according to God's commandments and to follow the daily leading of the Holy Spirit. The Holy Spirit helps us walk in this new way of life.

How does the Holy Spirit help us to live godly lives?

How might uncertainties of eternal security interfere with that process?

What About Repentance?

The word *repent* means to have a change of mind. The Holy Spirit will cause a person to desire a change of mind and a change of behavior. Repentance comes in the wake of salvation.

Let me give you an example of this. A man might have a change of mind about whether smoking is the right thing to do. He might begin to believe that smoking is harmful to his physical health and make a decision to change his behavior. In effect, he has "repented" of smoking. But this does not mean that this man is saved spiritually. Nothing about his sin nature has been altered, only his behavior has changed.

Many people walk down church aisles to kneel at altars and repent of behaviors that they know are bad or sinful in God's eyes. They repent of adulterous affairs, selfish actions, hateful words and deeds, and countless other deeds of their past. They believe that, by admitting their sins and making a promise to God, they are going to do "better" in the future, and they believe that they are then "saved." In reality, nothing has happened to them spiritually because they have not truly accepted and believed in Jesus as their sole means of salvation from the consequences of their sin nature. They may be confessing their sins, asking for forgiveness, and repenting, but they are not necessarily believing in and receiving Jesus Christ. A person can say, "I'm sorry, please forgive me, I don't ever want to do this again," and never say with genuine belief, "I believe in and accept what Jesus Christ did on the cross for my sins. I receive Him as my Savior."

Being good enough is not what brings about a new spiritual birth in a person. Salvation is solely a matter of *believing in Jesus*. The changes of behavior come later as the Holy Spirit prompts them, and also as the Holy Spirit helps a person to accomplish it! We will discuss this further in another lesson, but it is vitally important for you at this point to come to this understanding: Nothing that you do *apart from believing in Jesus Christ* causes you to be saved. When you believe, the Spirit enters into you and causes your old sin nature to be transformed into a new nature that is in the likeness of God. The transformation of your spirit is a sovereign work of God; you cannot make it happen by any means other than believing.

❧ When have you repented of a behavior and attempted to change, only to fall back into an old pattern? How did you feel? What did you do?

> For by grace you have been saved through faith, and that not of yourselves; it is the gift of God, not of works, lest anyone should boast.
>
> —Ephesians 2:8-9

❧ How might trying to change our behavior fall into the category of "works"? When is good behavior *not* a matter of works?

❧ Give some examples of how a person might "boast" if he were able to earn salvation by good works.

How Does This Relate to Eternal Security?

If you believe that your salvation came about by anything other than simply believing in what Jesus Christ did for you on the cross, then you believe that your salvation was in some way related to your own works. If you believe that your salvation is related to your works, then you will believe that you can in some way "undo" your salvation. On the other hand, if you believe that your salvation was based solely on what Jesus did for you and what the Holy Spirit has done in you, then you believe that your salvation was a sovereign work of God. Your part was simply to believe and receive what *God* provided and what *God* promised. We did absolutely nothing to transform our old sin nature into a new spiritual nature, and we cannot do anything to cause our new spiritual nature to revert to the old nature.

The critical questions are these:

❦ Have you believed in Jesus as the sole, substitutionary, atoning sacrifice for your sin nature?

❦ Have you yielded to the Holy Spirit in your life?

❦ Has the Holy Spirit transformed you and caused your spirit to be "reborn"?

If you cannot answer "yes" with full assurance today, then I invite you to look upon the death of Jesus and to believe in Him today. Receive Him as your Savior. You may want to pray this prayer or a similar one. The words are not important. What is important is the intent of your heart—to *believe in and receive* Jesus as Savior.

Lord, I acknowledge that I have a sin nature. No matter what I do or try, I cannot change this nature on my own. I acknowledge that my sin nature has separated me from You. Today, I look upon the cross of Jesus Christ, and I believe that Jesus is the substitutionary, atoning sacrifice for *my* sin nature. I acknowledge Him as my Savior. And I receive, as an act of my believing, the promises that You have made: I receive Your promise of everlasting life. I receive Your promise that my spirit will be "reborn" by the Holy Spirit and that the Holy Spirit from this moment on will live in me to transform my nature and my life. Thank You for sending Jesus to die in my place. Thank You for loving me enough to want to live with me forever.

And you He made alive, who were dead in trespasses and sins, in which you once walked according to the course of this world, according to the prince of the power of the air, the spirit who now works in the sons of disobedience, among whom also we all once conducted ourselves in the lusts of our flesh, fulfilling the desires of the flesh and of the mind, and were by nature children of wrath, just as the others.

—Ephesians 2:1-3

What does it mean to be "dead in trespasses and sins"? How does this "dead" condition change when we become born again?

🔊 Jesus promises that those who believe in Him gain eternal life. If we gain eternal life after being "dead in sin," what does that suggest about eternal security?

> Not by works of righteousness which we have done, but according to His mercy He saved us, through the washing of regeneration and renewing of the Holy Spirit, whom He poured out on us abundantly through Jesus Christ our Savior.

—Titus 3:5-6

🔊 What is the "washing of regeneration"? Why do we need the Holy Spirit to accomplish this?

🔊 Today and Tomorrow 🔊

TODAY: THE HOLY SPIRIT IS THE ONE WHO BRINGS "NEW BIRTH" TO A PERSON, MAKING HIM BE BORN AGAIN INTO THE LIFE OF CHRIST.

TOMORROW: I WILL PRAYERFULLY WORK AT YIELDING MY LIFE TO THE HOLY SPIRIT'S LEADING.

LESSON 3

Why Eternal Security is Important

✍ In This Lesson ✍

LEARNING: WHAT HAPPENS TO MY SALVATION IF I KEEP ON SINNING?

GROWING: HOW CAN I EVER HOPE TO FIND FREEDOM FROM SINFUL HABITS?

∽

A person's belief on eternal security is vitally important for several reasons, which we will cover in this lesson.

Knowing that You are Saved

First and foremost is the issue of whether a person can *know* that he is saved. The person who doesn't know with certainty that he is saved eternally is a person who frequently wonders whether he is saved at all. Many Christians wonder whether they have already lost their salvation. They say, "Oh, I know I was saved 'back then,' but I've sinned so much since then that I'm not really certain that I'm still saved." Such a person very likely thinks that he was saved by something other than believing, and there is something that he can do to "undo" his salvation.

The question is, can any person ever know with certainty whether he is saved or lost? Jesus said that we *can* know. In the Gospel of John (John 10:2–5, 16) we read:

But he who enters by the door is the shepherd of the sheep. To him the doorkeeper opens, and the sheep hear his voice; and he calls his own sheep by name and leads them out. And when he brings out his own sheep, he goes before them; and the sheep follow him, for they know his voice. Yet they will by no means follow a stranger, but will flee from him, for they do not know the voice of strangers. . . . Other sheep I have which are not of this fold; them also I must bring, and they will hear My voice; and there will be one flock and one shepherd.

The inner witness of the Holy Spirit will always assure the believer that he is a forgiven child of God, in right standing with the Father. The person who does not believe in the eternal security of his salvation has doubts about salvation and also has a certain amount of doubt about God, and especially about God's love, mercy, and ability to forgive. God wants you to *know* that you are eternally secure and that He is a loving, forgiving God whose mercy is without end. (See Lam. 3:22–24.)

☙ When have you questioned God's ability to forgive you, or to someone that you regard as a "repeat" sinner?

...It is the Spirit who bears witness, because the Spirit is truth.

—1 John 5:6

☙ What does it mean that "the Spirit is truth"?

22

How does the Spirit "bear witness" to us of our eternal security?

How Long will Salvation Last?

Those who believe that salvation is a temporary thing—that it can come and go, and come and go again, repeatedly—must answer the question, "For how long, then, is a person saved?"

As Long as We Don't Sin?

Is a person saved only as long as he doesn't sin? Surely not, since none of us can live in our earthly bodies without being subject to temptation and sin. Paul made it very clear that "all have sinned," and even though the Holy Spirit lives within us, we remain fleshly beings who often do what we don't want to do. Paul wrote about this in Romans 7:22–25:

> For I delight in the law of God according to the inward man. But I see another law in my members, warring against the law of my mind, and bringing me into captivity to the law of sin which is in my members. O wretched man that I am! Who will deliver me from this body of death? I thank God—through Jesus Christ our Lord! So then, with the mind I myself serve the law of God, but with the flesh the law of sin.

What "law of sin" is "in our members"? Give practical examples of how our flesh brings temptation.

When have you experienced such a "war" between your mind and flesh? What did you do? How did God help you with this?

The fact is, we are all going to sin after we are saved. We live in fallen bodies, in a fallen world, and we are not yet made perfect in Christ. Each of us will make mistakes, even though it is our hearts' desire that we be perfect in Christ Jesus and obey God in all ways. It simply is not possible for any person to live an error-free, mistake-free, sin-free life every minute of every day. The grace of God extends forgiveness to us even when we sin and fall short of God's perfect plan. (See Rom. 3:23 and 5:8.)

This, however, should not be taken as an excuse for sin! The person who truly knows Jesus as Savior will not want to sin and will sorrow at the thought that he has sinned. Nor are we protected from the consequences of the sin that we commit. We are very unwise to say, "Well, that's just the way I am. God knows that, so God won't punish me when I sin. I can't help myself."

You *can* help yourself! You can ask the Holy Spirit to help you withstand the temptation that seems to hound you. You can rely upon the Holy Spirit to give you the strength and courage that you need to live a pure life. It is within your capacity to be transformed so that you no longer have a desire to sin, so that you feel uncomfortable when you are around sin. Rather than say, "I can't help myself," we should be quick to say, "The Lord will help me" and quick to pray, "Lord, help me!" We must trust Christ to do for us what we cannot do ourselves. (See Phil. 4:13.)

We must never take God's grace for granted. Rather, we should thank and praise God that He is merciful toward us, patient with us, and faithful to us.

> I can do all things through Christ who strengthens me.
>
> —Philippians 4:13

How does this promise apply to resisting sin and temptation? How does a Christian "tap into" that power of Christ?

∞ How Many Times? ∞

How many times does Jesus have to die? How many times can a person be born again? The answer surely should be immediate in every Christian's mind: "Only once!" The apostle Paul, "The death that He died, He died to sin once for all" (Rom. 6:10). Yet those who believe that they can lose what Christ obtained on the cross seem to put themselves into a position of crucifying Him again and again. They act as if the death of Jesus were not sufficient the first time; therefore, they go to the Cross again and again.

Christ's death on the cross was definitive, and the work of the Holy Spirit is also definitive, bringing about a new spiritual "birth" to the person who believes in Jesus as Savior. Another way of asking this same question would be, "How many times does the Holy Spirit 're-birth' a person?" Only once! A person cannot physically return to the womb after being born, nor can we undo a spiritual new-birth experience once we have been born again by the power of the Holy Spirit. You cannot "kill" the Holy Spirit within you, regardless of what you do!

Wherever the Holy Spirit dwells, He brings eternal life because His own life is eternal. When the Holy Spirit dwells in your spirit, He brings His eternal life to your spirit. He does not depart, now or forever. (See Rom. 8:9–11.)

> And if Christ is in you, the body is dead because of sin, but the Spirit is life because of righteousness. But if the Spirit of Him who raised Jesus from the dead dwells in you, He who raised Christ from the dead will also give life to your mortal bodies through His Spirit who dwells in you.

> —Romans 8:10-11

∾ Why do we still feel temptation if "the body is dead"?

∾ According to these verses, how can the Holy Spirit help us resist temptation?

∞ Was Christ's Death Sufficient? ∞

Those who believe that they can fall from grace cite their ongoing sin as the means by which they fall. Questions naturally arise:

- How much sin?

- How frequent a sin?

- How long will God be patient before He negates salvation?

These questions have no answer in Scripture because they are the wrong questions to be asking! Once you have accepted Jesus Christ as your Savior, your sin cannot undo your salvation. You simply cannot "evict" the Holy Spirit from a heart that He has chosen to indwell. To say that you can negate your salvation by your sin is to say that Christ's death on the cross was not sufficient for your salvation in the first place. It is to say that something else had to be done to earn salvation. Christ's death was sufficient to pay your sin debt in *full*.

Why do people continue to pay for the free salvation that Jesus has granted to them? I believe the main reason is pride. People want to think that they have earned what they have. We are reluctant receivers. Nevertheless, a "receiver" is precisely the position that we are in. Is it "cheap salvation" because all that is required of us is our belief to receive a free gift of God? No! Our salvation cost Jesus' life! Our salvation is expensive salvation, but it is salvation that is offered to us as a precious gift. We must never take salvation lightly, but at the same time there is nothing that we can do to deserve it.

The simple truth is this: you can't pay for your salvation, either before or after you receive it. Christ already paid for it.

27

...A man is not justified by the works of the law but by faith in Jesus Christ, even we have believed in Christ Jesus, that we might be justified by faith in Christ and not by the works of the law; for by the works of the law no flesh shall be justified.

—Galatians 2:16

🔊 In what way are we actually trusting in "the works of the law" when we doubt that we have eternal security?

The Impact on Your Daily Life

What you believe about eternal security has a direct bearing on your daily life. If you believe that your salvation can be "lost," then you will take one of two positions:

1. You will be constantly striving to "keep" your salvation, which often ends in great anxiety and a false sense of righteousness, or

2. You will feel the futility of your efforts—a feeling of frustration and despair—because eventually you will be forced to face the fact that you have not led a sin-free life since you believed in Christ.

The person who strives to earn his salvation is a person who will lose his joy. He also may eventually lose his hope. The person who feels that he simply cannot maintain a sin-free life will eventually question God's desire to forgive. An even deeper issue, however, is that God does not want you to live in this state. He wants you to know that He has forgiven you, and that He is working within you to transform your life into the image of Christ Jesus. God will deal with your sin and use it to train you in the ways of righteousness, but He does not strip away your salvation or your heavenly home in the process!

The Impact on Your Witness

Believing that you can fall from God's grace affects your daily life, and it affects your witness for Jesus Christ. If you believe that you can lose your salvation, how will you convince another person to be born again? If you believe that you are only saved as long as you remain sin-free, what kind of "blessed assurance" can you offer to another person in Christ Jesus?

Those who believe that a person can fall from grace often have a very difficult time motivating themselves to witness actively about Jesus Christ. Any salesman knows that it is extremely difficult to make sales calls if he is selling a bad product. The same is true for the gospel. Either it is the supremely good news of eternal salvation, or it is a flawed provision that requires the futile efforts of man.

In sharp contrast, those who believe that they are eternally secure tend to have an exuberance in witnessing. They are offering a glorious salvation, a truly wonderful gift of God to the sinner. They know that it is Jesus who saves and the Holy Spirit who indwells, and they know that a believer becomes God's own child to train, nurture, and love—forever! What a tremendous future we have been given!

And there are three that bear witness on earth: the Spirit, the
water, and the blood; and these three agree as one.... He who
believes in the Son of God has the witness in himself; he who
does not believe God has made Him a liar, because he has not
believed the testimony that God has given of His Son.... These
things I have written to you who believe in the name of the Son
of God, that you may know that you have eternal life, and that
you may continue to believe in the name of the Son of God.

—1 John 5:8, 10, 13

What "water" and "blood" is John referring to here? How do
they "bear witness" of our eternal security in Christ?

How do we "make God a liar" when we don't have faith in our
eternal security?

My little children, these things I write to you, so that you may not sin. And if anyone sins, we have an Advocate with the Father, Jesus Christ the righteous. And He Himself is the propitiation for our sins, and not for ours only but also for the whole world.

—1 John 2:1–2

❧ What does it mean that Jesus is our "Advocate"?

❧ What does this role imply about God's attitude toward sin?

❧ Today and Tomorrow ❧

TODAY: GOD TAKES SIN SERIOUSLY, BUT HE ALSO PROVIDES US WITH HIS HOLY SPIRIT—WHO FREES US FROM SIN.

TOMORROW: I WILL ASK GOD TO SHOW ME HOW MY ATTITUDE TOWARD ETERNAL SECURITY IS AFFECTING MY LIFE AND MY WITNESS FOR HIM.

LESSON 4

Seven Reasons to Believe in Eternal Security

Part 1

❧ In This Lesson ❧

LEARNING: WILL I LOSE MY SALVATION IF I FALL INTO SIN?

GROWING: HOW DO I KNOW THAT JESUS WILL ALWAYS WANT ME?

Security is important. We all long to be financially secure, to have secure homes, and to enjoy personal safety and security. Our spiritual security, however, is the most precious type of security that we can know. The Scriptures provide seven overriding reasons for believing in eternal security. We will deal with three of them in this lesson:

1. The omnipotence and omnipresence of God

2. The continuing intercession of Christ on our behalf

3. The prevailing love of Christ

God's Omnipotence and Omnipresence

The first great reason for believing in eternal security lies in the very nature of God. What we believe about our salvation is related to what we believe about God. Many people seem to think that God and the devil are on an equal plane—God is on the side of good, the devil is on the side of bad—and mankind is between the two, caught in something of a great tug-of-war between opposite but equal forces. That is *not* what the Bible teaches.

God is sovereign. He is the Almighty One, the King of the universe. The devil is totally subject to God's authority; he operates only within the boundaries that God defines. God is victor over the devil in any conflict.

The devil—once the archangel Lucifer—fell from God's presence in heaven through his rebellion against God. The devil attempts to trick people into believing that they will also fall from God's presence any time they sin. That is true for mankind as a whole—we are born with a sin nature because of the "fall" of Adam and Eve—but it is *not* true for the person who has believed in Jesus Christ and received the gift of eternal life. Such a person is firmly established—*with* God, *in* God, and inseparable *from* God. That person cannot fall away from God, nor can the devil snatch him away from God in a tug-of-war contest.

Consider these unchanging attributes of God:

&. *God does not lie.* His Word is true. The devil is the liar. (See John 8:44.)

&. *God cannot be defeated by the devil or by any human being.* The devil is a defeated foe, eternally defeated by Jesus' death on the cross. (See 1 Cor. 15:57.)

❧ *God does not change, regardless of how a human being may change.* The devil is the one who appears in many disguises. (See Heb. 13:8.)

❧ *God cannot be avoided, escaped, or removed by any act or will of man.* We can, however, resist the devil so that he will flee from us. (See James 4:7.)

God is supreme and infinite. The devil is subject to God and is finite. These attributes of God's nature are especially important in the light of our relationship with God. Once we have believed in Jesus Christ and received Him as our Savior, we enter a lasting relationship with God. The shed blood of Jesus has qualified us fully for this relationship; God is the author of the relationship and His presence begins to abide with us in a way that transforms us. *We are eternally in His grip!* Nothing that the devil can say or do alters our position or destroys our relationship with God.

The psalmist wrote, "The LORD is my shepherd; I shall not want" (Ps. 23:1). As a sheep of the Lord, David recognized that God provided rest, nourishment, guidance, protection, blessing, and a full restoration of soul. He concluded, "Surely goodness and mercy shall follow me all the days of my life; and I will dwell in the house of the LORD forever" (Ps. 23:6). At no time does the psalmist remotely indicate that his relationship with the Lord is tentative, subject to being broken, or that he can cease being a sheep in God's fold.

Jesus echoed this when He said, "I am the good shepherd" (John 10:11). Later in the Gospel of John (John 17:6–12, 20–21), Jesus prayed for His disciples:

> I have manifested Your name to the men whom You have given Me out of the world. They were Yours, You gave them to Me, and they have kept Your word. Now they have known that all

things which You have given Me are from You. For I have given
to them the words which You have given Me; and they have
received them, and have known surely that I came forth from
You; and they have believed that You sent Me. I pray for them.
I do not pray for the world but for those whom You have given
Me, for they are Yours. And all Mine are Yours, and Yours are
Mine, and I am glorified in them. . . . Keep through Your name
those whom You have given Me, that they may be one as We
are. While I was with them in the world, I kept them in Your
name. Those whom You gave Me I have kept; and none of them
is lost except the son of perdition, that the Scripture might be
fulfilled. . . . I do not pray for these alone, but also for those
who will believe in Me through their word; that they all may be
one, as You, Father, are in Me, and I in You; that they also may
be one in Us, that the world may believe that You sent Me.

Note that Jesus hasn't lost a single disciple that the Father gave to Him.
Neither has the Father ever lost a soul that has believed in Jesus Christ.
When we are reunited to God through the blood of Jesus Christ, we
are inseparable from God. We become "one" with Him. We cannot be
snatched or pried away from Him. His omnipotence (all powerful nature) assures that no power can rip us away from His love and care.

Our eternal security lies in the fact that God is undefeatable and always
present. He knows all, sees all, and is victorious over all. Nothing can
take Him by surprise or catch Him off guard. He cannot be tricked,
manipulated, or conned. The devil and all the demons of hell cannot
steal you away from His eternal grasp.

If God is for us, who can be against us?

—Romans 8:31

🙘 What has God done on your behalf which prove the He is "for you"?

🙘 How does this truth strengthen your belief in eternal security?

Christ's Intercession for Us

In the New Testament we read that Jesus Christ is presently seated at the right hand of God the Father, where He is interceding or "advocating" for us. What is it that Jesus is praying for us in heaven? Very likely it is the same prayer that we find in John 17:15–19, 24:

I do not pray that You should take them out of the world, but that You should keep them from the evil one. They are not of the world, just as I am not of the world. Sanctify them by Your truth. Your word is truth. As You sent Me into the world, I also have sent them into the world. And for their sakes I sanctify Myself, that they also may be sanctified by the truth.... Father, I desire that they also whom You gave Me may be with Me where I am, that they may behold My glory which You have given Me; for You loved Me before the foundation of the world.

Jesus is praying that we will be delivered from evil, be victorious witnesses to the gospel of Jesus Christ, and behold the glory of Jesus. What a wonderful prayer is being made on your behalf every moment since you believed on Jesus Christ and received Him as your Savior! Do you think that God the Father will fail to answer the prayer of His Son—even for an instant?

Jesus' prayer for us is about our relationship with Him and with the Father. We certainly sin and make mistakes, but Jesus' intercession for us will bring about our chastening so that our eternal relationship with the Father might become even stronger and more intimate. Jesus' prayer attests to the permanence of our relationship "in God" so that we become "one" with Him and with Christ. With Jesus praying this, how dare we believe that we can in any way negate, abolish, or supersede His prayer?

Who shall bring a charge against God's elect? It is God who justifies. Who is he who condemns? It is Christ who died, and furthermore is also risen, who is even at the right hand of God, who also makes intercession for us.

—Romans 8:33-34

⊷ When has someone "brought a charge" against you? Was it true or false? Did anyone "intercede" on your behalf?

⊷ Satan frequently brings charges against us before God. How do you know that Jesus will intercede on your behalf? How do you know that He'll "win"?

> My little children, these things I write to you, so that you may not sin. And if anyone sins, we have an Advocate with the Father, Jesus Christ the righteous.
>
> —1 John 2:1

⊷ What does this verse tell us about our struggle against sin?

⊷ What encouragement do you find in this verse?

The Prevailing Love of Christ

One of the most stirring and comforting passages of the entire New Testament is Romans 8:35–39:

> Who shall separate us from the love of Christ? Shall tribulation, or distress, or persecution, or famine, or nakedness, or peril, or sword? As it is written: *"For Your sake we are killed all day long; We are accounted as sheep for the slaughter."* Yet in all these things we are more than conquerors through Him who loved us. For I am persuaded that neither death nor life, nor angels nor principalities nor powers, nor things present nor things to come, nor height nor depth, nor any other created thing, shall be able to separate us from the love of God which is in Christ Jesus our Lord.

Paul makes this statement just after he told the Romans, "We know that all things work together for good to those who love God, to those who are the called according to His purpose. For whom He foreknew, He also predestined to be conformed to the image of His Son, that He might be the firstborn among many brethren. Moreover whom He predestined, these He also called; whom He called, these He also justified; and whom He justified, these He also glorified" (Rom. 8:28–30).

Paul's statement about Christ's love is for those who are:

 The beloved who have been called according to God's purpose: those who have believed in Jesus and received God's gift of forgiveness and everlasting life.

 The justified: those who are no longer guilty in their sins but have been declared righteous because of their belief in Jesus, who paid their sin debt in full.

39

🕮 *The glorified:* those who will partake of Christ's eternal glory, bound and identified with Him so that we reflect the glory of His nature.

Paul asks three questions related to our position in Christ's love:

1. Who can accuse us and make it stick? (See Rom. 8:33.)

2. Who can condemn us and make us guilty? (See Rom. 8:34.)

3. Who can separate us from Christ? (See Rom. 8:35.)

The answer is the same to all three questions: nothing and nobody! No event or state of being can destroy the prevailing power of Christ's love in our lives. There is no person or demonic power that can destroy Christ's love for us. There is no time in which we are separated from His love. There is nothing in heaven or hell that can pry us from His love! Christ's love for us is a shield that cannot be penetrated, removed, or deactivated!

> In this is love, not that we loved God, but that He loved us and sent His Son to be the propitiation for our sins. Beloved, if God so loved us, we also ought to love one another.

> —1 John 4:10-11

🕮 Propitiation means to appease, to satisfy God's sense of justice. How did Christ's death and resurrection accomplish this on your behalf?

40

🖎 If God's outrage against your sin is fully satisfied, how does this affect any "charges" that are brought against you in the future? How does it affect your eternal security?

If ever a person deserved to be estranged from Christ, it was Peter, who denied knowing Jesus three times at the most stressful period of His earthly life. Yet Jesus appeared to Peter after the Resurrection and asked him three times, "Do you love Me?" (See John 21:15–19.) Jesus allowed Peter to declare his love for the Lord just as many times as he had denied it earlier. What was *never* in question, however, was Jesus' love for Peter! That remained constant and prevailing—it was not even dented by what Peter had done or failed to do.

We sometimes doubt that God can love us, but what we are really doubting is whether we are worthy of God's love. God is the One who declares that we are worthy to love. He is the One who found us so worthy to love that He sent His only begotten Son, Jesus Christ, to die on a cross in our place. We do not determine our worthiness; God does! And He says to each of us, "I love you with an immeasurable, everlasting love." It is up to us to receive what God gives. As John wrote, "We love Him because He first loved us" (1 John 4:19).

What should be our response to Christ's prevailing love, which keeps us in an inseparable relationship with Him? To love Him back! To thank and praise Him for His great love. And, as John also wrote, "to love one another" (1 John 4:11).

Paul wrote eloquently about love in 1 Corinthians 13. Very often we think of this chapter as pertaining only to human love—the love of one person for another person. At times we may think of it as relating to our love for God. Read the following verses from 1 Corinthians, and think in terms of God loving *you*. The love that we have for others is born first of God's great love for us.

> Love suffers long and is kind; love does not envy; love does not parade itself, is not puffed up; does not behave rudely, does not seek its own, is not provoked, thinks no evil; does not rejoice in iniquity, but rejoices in the truth; bears all things, believes all things, hopes all things, endures all things. Love never fails.
>
> —1 Corinthians 13:4-8

🖎 Go through the qualities of love one at a time, and give practical examples of each.

🖎 God is love (1 John 4:8, 16), and "love never fails." How does this affect your eternal security?

And Jesus came and spoke to them, saying, "All authority has been given to Me in heaven and on earth.... And lo, I am with you always, even to the end of the age." Amen.

—Matthew 28:18, 20

❧ What types of "authority" does Jesus have? Give practical examples. How does His authority guarantee your eternal security?

Therefore He is also able to save to the uttermost those who come to God through Him, since He always lives to make intercession for them.

—Hebrews 7:25

❧ What does it mean that Jesus is "able to save to the uttermost"? Why not just "He is able to save"?

❧ Why does Jesus make intercession for us? Why do we need someone to intercede with God on our behalf?

❧ Today and Tomorrow ❧

TODAY: JESUS IS MY FAITHFUL ADVOCATE, ALWAYS INTERCEDING AND DEFENDING ME.

TOMORROW: I WILL ASK HIM TO TEACH ME TO LOVE OTHERS THE WAY THAT HE LOVES ME.

❧ Notes and Prayer Requests: ❧

LESSON 5

Seven Reasons to Believe in Eternal Security

Part 2

❧ In This Lesson ❧

LEARNING: WHAT HAPPENS IF I BACKSLIDE? CAN I REVERSE MY SALVATION?

GROWING: HOW DOES THE HOLY SPIRIT MAKE A DIFFERENCE IN MY ETERNAL SECURITY?

The apostle Peter wrote, "Always be ready to give a defense to everyone who asks you a reason for the hope that is in you" (1 Peter 3:15). Certainly nothing gives a person more cause for hope than to know that he is saved from the consequences of his sin nature by believing in Jesus Christ, and that he has an everlasting relationship with God and a home in heaven. What reasons might we give for having such a hope?

In the last lesson, we covered three reasons for believing in eternal security. In this lesson, we will deal with four additional reasons:

1. God's eternal purpose for us

2. The irreversible nature of our new life in Christ

3. The binding nature of the Holy Spirit's "seal" on our lives

4. The faithfulness of God

God's Eternal Purpose for Us

In the last lesson we cited Paul's words to the Romans: "For whom He foreknew, He also predestined to be conformed to the image of His Son, that He might be the firstborn among many brethren. Moreover whom He predestined, these He also called; whom He called, these He also justified; and whom He justified, these He also glorified" (Rom. 8:29–30).

I want to call your attention to two main things about this brief passage. First, God's purpose for you is a total "conformation" to the image of His Son, Jesus Christ. To be conformed to something is to become like it in all essential ways. God's purpose for each of us is that we talk like Jesus—we say what Jesus would say if He were in our situation. We respond like Jesus—we do what He would do if He were facing our circumstances. We act boldly with love and power in any situation where we find need, sickness, or pain.

Jesus sent out His disciples, telling them, "As you go, preach, saying, 'The kingdom of heaven is at hand.' Heal the sick, cleanse the lepers, raise the dead, cast out demons. Freely you have received, freely give" (Matt. 10:7–8). The disciples were given power over unclean spirits, to cast them out, and to heal all kinds of sickness and all kinds of disease. (See Matt. 10:1.) This is a portrait of conformation. The disciples were conformed to the nature and the likeness of Jesus. What they did, we are expected to do today as we are conformed to Him through the power of the Holy Spirit. The Holy Spirit has been given to all who believe in Jesus and receive Him as Savior so that we might be Christ's ambassadors in our world today.

🐾 What does it mean, in practical terms, to be "conformed to the image of Christ Jesus"?

🐾 What areas of your own life need to conform more? What areas are becoming conformed now?

Second, God's conformation process has four progressive and irreversible stages: predestined, called, justified, and glorified. Our conformation begins with the fact that God has predestined us for this process. God's purpose for your creation, birth, and ongoing life on this earth is that He might conform you into the nature of Christ and live with you forever. He called you, and you came to accept Jesus as your Savior. In accepting Jesus, you were justified by God so that you were no longer held bound by your sin nature. In being justified, you are in the process of being glorified.

These four stages proceed naturally and normally without variation in the life of every person who comes to believe in Jesus Christ as Savior. There are no variations on this theme, no alternate routes, no different processes. You were predestined to be called; you were called in order to be justified; you were justified to be glorified.

It is folly to think it remotely possible that we can reverse this God-ordained process. You cannot go from being justified back to being un-called!

∽ How have you seen these stages of progression in your own life?

∽ In what areas do you need to see more progression?

The third thing to note in this passage is that all four words are in the past tense. Most of us think that we will be glorified one day, and those who believe that it is possible to fall from grace say that we *might* be glorified if we continue to live the right way. But Paul writes about our glorification as an accomplished fact. It's a "done deal." The progression is irreversible, and every believer *will* be glorified.

Once you enter God's conformation process through believing in Jesus Christ, nothing that you or anyone else can do will reverse that process or keep it from happening. God *will* justify and glorify you. The good work that has begun in you will continue and eventually be completed because the One doing the work is God!

...looking unto Jesus, the author and finisher of our faith, who for the joy that was set before Him endured the cross, despising the shame, and has sat down at the right hand of the throne of God.

—Hebrews 12:2

❧ What does it mean that Jesus is "the author and finisher of our faith"?

❧ Note that the roles of "author" and "finisher" are inseparable in this verse. What does that tell you about your eternal security?

An Irreversible New Nature

In an earlier lesson we asked the question, "How can a person who is born physically reenter the womb and become 'unborn'?" It isn't possible. Neither is it possible for a person who has been spiritually reborn to become spiritually "unborn." When a person is born physically, he enters a completely new dimension of being. He breathes in the atmosphere of the earth and, from that moment on, he is dependent upon oxygen. He cannot live without oxygen for more than a few minutes. Thus, he can never return to an existence of living in the fluid of his mother's body.

This is also true for us spiritually. Once we have believed in Jesus Christ and received salvation, we are filled with the Spirit of God and we cannot undo that "new state" in which we find ourselves. From that moment on, we live and move and have our being in Christ Jesus. (See Acts 17:28.)

∞ New Creatures ∞

Paul wrote to the Corinthians that "if anyone is in Christ, he is a new creation; old things have passed away; behold, all things have become new" (2 Corinthians 5:17). The new creature is incapable of thinking and responding as the old creature did. The Holy Spirit begins to prick the conscience of the believer so that suddenly he sees life from a completely new perspective. Things that were not previously thought to be sins come to be seen as sins. Scales have been dropped from our eyes and we are able to see God, ourselves, our relationship with God, and all of life from a new point of view. We can never go back to a state of "not knowing," "not seeing," or "not understanding" because the very Spirit of Truth now lives in us. (See John 14:17.)

∞ Adopted Sons ∞

A third word that relates to our new state of being in Christ Jesus is *adoption*. Paul wrote, "For as many as are led by the Spirit of God, these are sons of God. For you did not receive the spirit of bondage again to fear, but you received the Spirit of adoption by whom we cry out, 'Abba, Father'" (Rom. 8:14–15).

In the ancient world, the child who was adopted actually had more rights than a child born into a family. A father could give up his natural-born child to adoption, but a child once adopted could never be given up again. It was illegal to do so. A natural-born child could be expelled from the family, disowned, or denied. An adopted child, however, could not be dissociated from the father who had adopted him.

Paul was well aware of the legal rights and ramifications of adoption when he wrote that believers in Christ Jesus are full partakers of "the adoption, the glory, the covenants, the giving of the law, the service of God, and the promises" once thought to be available only to the Jews (Rom. 9:4). Believers in Christ Jesus are not second-class members of the family of God but full sons of the Almighty! (See Gal. 4:4–7 and Eph. 1:3–5.)

Can a person who has been born become "unborn"? No. Can a new creation be "unmade" and become an old creation? No. Can a child adopted by God become "unadopted"? No. Each of these word pictures alludes to an irreversible state of being. What God transforms cannot be "undone" or "untransformed." Having entered a new spiritual state, we are in that state throughout the rest of our lives and into eternity.

> But when the fullness of the time had come, God sent forth His Son, born of a woman, born under the law, to redeem those who were under the law, that we might receive the adoption as sons. And because you are sons, God has sent forth the Spirit of His Son into your hearts, crying out, "Abba, Father!" Therefore you are no longer a slave but a son, and if a son, then an heir of God through Christ.
>
> —Galatians 4:4-7

☙ Describe God's relationship with His Son, Jesus. As an adopted son of God, you also share that relationship. How does this affect your thinking on eternal security?

☙ "Abba, Father" might be translated "Daddy! Daddy!" This is the cry of the Holy Spirit, who lives within you. What does this suggest about your eternal security?

The irreversible nature of our new lives as sons of God is portrayed in the story told by Jesus about a loving father and a prodigal son. (See Luke 15:11–32.) At no time in this story do we find any indication that the prodigal son *ceased* to belong to his father's family. He went as far away from his father as he could go, wasted his possessions and his inheritance, and fell to a point of near starvation slopping pigs for a pagan—yet, even then, this prodigal son was welcomed home by his father without any sign of rejection or alienation, and without any condemnation. The prodigal son lost a great deal in his sin—his status, his health, his possessions—but he did *not* lose his relationship with his father. He was always his father's son, and the father moved quickly upon the boy's return to restore to him the visible marks of sonship: sandals, a cloak, and a ring.

The same is true for us. Regardless of what we may do after we become a child of God through Christ Jesus (see Eph. 1:5), we do not lose our relationship with God. He remains our loving, forgiving heavenly Father, always available to us with open arms. We are His children forever.

Read Luke 15:11–31.

What does this parable teach you about eternal security?

In what ways have you been like the prodigal son? Are you still "slopping pigs" now, or have you returned to the Father?

The Sure Seal of the Holy Spirit

Paul wrote to the Ephesians that believers have been "sealed with the Holy Spirit of promise, who is the guarantee of our inheritance until the redemption of the purchased possession, to the praise of His glory" (Eph. 1:13–14).

What does it mean to be "sealed"? In the ancient world, a seal upon an item meant two things. First, the item was linked to a specific owner. Seals bore markings that indicated to whom the object belonged, from whom it had been sent, or by whom it had been purchased. To be sealed by the Holy Spirit is an indication that we are now "owned" by God the Father for His purposes.

A seal also meant that an item was authentic. Seals were rarely forged because each seal was handmade, and variations were easily spotted. When we are sealed by the Holy Spirit, the Holy Spirit "authenticates" our conversion experience. The Holy Spirit becomes the witness to the fact that we have believed in Jesus.

Once the Holy Spirit indwells us, the very presence of the Holy Spirit is a "living seal" that we are God's children, fully authentic as heirs of Christ. Nobody and nothing can undo the seal of the Holy Spirit in the life of a believer. As Paul wrote to the Corinthians, we are no longer our own. Our bodies are members of Christ's body. The spirit within us is Christ's Spirit. We belong to God. (See 1 Corinthians 6:15, 17, 19–20.)

Paul wrote to the Ephesians that the Holy Spirit is a seal "of promise." What is this promise? It is "the guarantee of our inheritance until the redemption of the purchased possession" (Eph. 1:13–14). In other words, the Holy Spirit seals us until the day when God greets us face-to-face in heaven and we are secure in His presence there forever. Our full redemption is accomplished the day that we enter God's glory in heaven. Until then, the Holy Spirit is the firm "guarantee" that this redemption *will* take place.

> In Him you also trusted, after you heard the word of truth, the gospel of your salvation; in whom also, having believed, you were sealed with the Holy Spirit of promise, who is the guarantee of our inheritance until the redemption of the purchased possession, to the praise of His glory.
>
> —Ephesians 1:13-14

✎ Explain in your own words what Paul is saying in these verses.

✎ What is the "inheritance" of those who are adopted into God's family?

God's Absolute Faithfulness

God does what He says He will do. At no time in the Scriptures do we find God failing to keep His word or fulfill His promises. Paul wrote about this to Timothy (2 Timothy 2:11–13):

> This is a faithful saying: For if we died with Him, we shall also live with Him. If we endure, we shall also reign with Him. If we deny Him, He also will deny us. If we are faithless, He remains faithful; He cannot deny Himself.

God does not change. He is the same yesterday, today, and forever. (See Hebrews 13:8.) In Him, there is no variance, no turning, no shadow. (See James 1:17.) Furthermore, God does not play favorites or show partiality to one person over another. What He has said or promised to one, He says and promises to all. (See Acts 10:34.) His word bears no mark of hypocrisy. (See James 3:17.)

The unchanging, steadfast, absolute nature of God makes Him utterly faithful and trustworthy. If God has said that we receive everlasting life when we believe in Jesus Christ, we can count on that being true! If God has extended the promise of eternal life to "whosoever believeth," then the promise is surely to all who believe! All of the promises and teachings that pertain to eternal security can be relied upon as *truth*. Ultimately, we need no other reason to believe in eternal security than this: God said that He gives eternal life to those who believe in Jesus Christ. What God says, God does.

But the Lord is faithful, who will establish you and guard you
from the evil one.

—2 Thessalonians 3:3

🐚 What does it mean that God "will establish you"? How does
being "established" affect your eternal security?

Being confident of this very thing, that He who has begun a
good work in you will complete it until the day of Jesus Christ;
... you all are partakers with me of grace.

—Philippians 1:6–7

🐚 Why is it important to God to finish the "good work in you"
which He began at your salvation? If it is so important to Him,
what does this mean regarding your eternal security?

🐚 What does it mean to be "partakers of grace"? How does this
grace affect your eternal security?

57

Blessed be the God and Father of our Lord Jesus Christ, who has blessed us with every spiritual blessing in the heavenly places in Christ, just as He chose us in Him before the foundation of the world, that we should be holy and without blame before Him in love, having predestined us to adoption as sons by Jesus Christ to Himself, according to the good pleasure of His will.

—Ephesians 1:3-5

🙝 When did God decide to adopt you as a son? How likely is it, therefore, that He will "unadopt" you?

🙝 According to this verse, what is God's motive in adopting men and women into His eternal family? What part does your "righteousness" play in this?

🙝 Today and Tomorrow 🙝

TODAY: GOD HAS HIMSELF SEALED MY SALVATION—PERMANENTLY—WITH HIS HOLY SPIRIT.

TOMORROW: I WILL PRAYERFULLY STRIVE TO BE AS FAITHFUL TO GOD AS HE IS TO ME.

LESSON 6

Solemn Warnings

Part 1

✎ In This Lesson ✎

Learning: But what if I have doubts about my salvation?

Growing: What does it mean to "fall from grace"?

∽∽∽

In the next two lessons, we are going to deal with some of the arguments that are put forward by those who believe that it is possible to "fall from grace"—which is to "lose" one's salvation or to backslide to the point of needing to be "saved again."

We need to recognize as we begin this portion of our study that the devil is the "accuser of our brethren" (Revelation 12:10). The devil accuses believers as well as unbelievers. In fact, John wrote that he accuses the brethren "before God day and night." He tries to claim that believers are not born again and that they are separated from God by their sin. Certainly the devil knows that, if he can keep Christians preoccupied with their own salvation, they will be far less effective in evangelism and other types of ministry. If the devil can plant doubts in a believer's mind regarding his eternal destiny, he can readily plant doubts about the nature of God, the nature of the relationship God desires with man, and the nature of the Holy Spirit's work within us.

Why Do We Doubt?

I believe there are two reasons for doubting eternal security. First, we continue to sin after we are saved and many Christians have not been taught properly regarding the difference between a sin nature (which separates man from God) and sinful acts (which can be committed by both believers and nonbelievers). We will discuss sin and its consequences in a later chapter.

Second, certain passages of Scripture seem to say on the surface that a person can "lose" his salvation. When one studies these passages in context and in the full depth of their meaning in comparison to other similar teachings, a picture emerges that strongly supports eternal security. We will focus on these passages in the next two lessons so that you might understand why some believe that we can fall from grace, and so that you will know how to respond to those who hold that position.

I believe that these passages serve as "solemn warnings" to the church. Their purpose is not to pass judgment or issue condemnation, but rather to teach, warn, and admonish believers on very particular issues.

"Fallen from Grace"

Paul wrote in Galatians 5:1–6:

> Stand fast therefore in the liberty by which Christ has made us free, and do not be entangled again with a yoke of bondage. Indeed I, Paul, say to you that if you become circumcised, Christ will profit you nothing. And I testify again to every man who becomes circumcised that he is a debtor to keep the whole law. You have become estranged from Christ, you who attempt to

be justified by law; you have fallen from grace. For we through
the Spirit eagerly wait for the hope of righteousness by faith.
For in Christ Jesus neither circumcision nor uncircumcision
avails anything, but faith working through love.

This passage often leads people to believe that they can fall from grace
since it uses the very phrase, "fallen from grace." We must be very careful to read this passage in the context of the entire book of Galatians,
and to have a clear understanding of the audience to whom Paul was
writing, if we are to understand its meaning.

Paul was writing primarily to churches that he founded on his mis-
sionary journeys. Some of the members of these churches were Jewish
Christians, while others were Gentiles who had come into the church.
Both Jews and Christians were influenced by the Greek and Roman
cultures, a fact that caused confusion in many of the new converts.

After their conversion to Christ, the Galatians were visited by people
called "Judaizers," who taught that a Christian Jew had to continue
to observe the Law of Moses. Furthermore, the Judaizers taught the
Gentile Christians that they needed to be circumcised and to follow the
Law of Moses and the traditions of Judaism. To the Judaizers, a person
could not be a Christian without also becoming a full-fledged Jew.

Paul disagreed strongly with the Judaizers. He wrote to the Galatians
for the purpose of saying very directly to them, "If you go back to the
old way of keeping the Law and assuming that you are in right standing with God *because* you keep the Law, you have totally negated what
Christ did on the cross. If you go back, you will render Christ's death
on the cross as being of no benefit to you." Another way of saying this
would have been, "If you return to the Law as your means of salvation,
why have Christ? Christ fulfilled the Law. He embodied the Law. To
believe in Christ is to believe in something that completes the Law.

Why live in the bondage of the Law, which does nothing but point out to you that you are a sinner in need of salvation, when you can live in the freedom of forgiveness made possible by Jesus Christ?"

Paul was a strong advocate that grace, and grace alone, was God's method of salvation through Jesus. No works of man were required in the salvation of a person's soul. God's love motivated Him to send Jesus; Jesus' death on the cross was the only requirement for atonement of sins; and believing on Jesus was the only thing necessary to receive God's forgiveness and gain eternal life.

Paul was *not* saying that the believers who returned to the Law were no longer covered by God's grace and forgiveness. Rather, he was saying that they had fallen away from God's provision of grace and bound themselves again to the constrictions of the Law. God had not cast them away; they had again taken upon themselves the yoke of the Law and had moved away from a position of grace.

> Stand fast therefore in the liberty by which Christ has made us free, and do not be entangled again with a yoke of bondage.
>
> —Galatians 5:1

⚫ What does it mean to become "entangled with a yoke of bondage"? Give practical examples of modern "yokes of bondage."

⚫ How can such things make you unsure of eternal security?

To What Do You Fall?

The question certainly arises, "What do you fall *to* if you can fall from grace?" The answer can only be, "To works." If you no longer accept the fact that simple belief in Jesus Christ is sufficient for everlasting life, then on what will you rely for your salvation? You will have to rely upon your good works. Paul says very clearly, "We through the Spirit eagerly wait for the hope of righteousness by faith" (Gal. 5:5). The Law won't provide what you are trusting it to provide, he says. Paul chooses instead to opt for *faith* as the means by which the Spirit puts a person into right standing with God (which is righteousness).

Paul goes on from these few verses to remind the brethren in Galatia that they have been called to *liberty*—not so they can sin, but so that they might love and serve one another. He challenges them to walk in the Spirit so that they won't fulfill the lusts of the flesh. He spells out clearly the lusts of the flesh and also the fruit of the Spirit. (See Gal. 5:19–25.)

If we live in the Spirit, let us also walk in the Spirit.

—Galatians 5:25

🔊 What does it mean to "live in the Spirit"? What does it mean to "walk in the Spirit"?

🔊 How does "walking in the Spirit" bring a clearer understanding of eternal security?

One of Two Paths

In summary, Paul sets before the believers two paths that they might take:

1. A path of the Law, which is filled with "don't do this, don't do that" commandments—a Law that points out man's sins and which is rooted in a concern with what *not* to do.

2. A path of grace, which is filled with "do this, do that" out of love for Christ—a path that points out the provision of the Holy Spirit to help us in right living, rooted in a freedom to do those things that are both pleasing to God and beneficial for life.

You cannot walk both paths simultaneously, Paul warns. If you walk the path of the Law, you will be turning your back on the path of grace. If you walk the path of grace, you will fulfill the Law but not be bound by it. At no time, however, does Paul indicate that these Galatians will lose their salvation. What they are in danger of losing is the joy of their salvation and the freedom of following the daily leading of the Holy Spirit!

"Blotted" from the Book of Life

In Revelation 3:1–5, we find this passage that is often used to support a belief in the ability of a believer to fall from grace:

And to the angel of the church in Sardis write, "These things says He who has the seven Spirits of God and the seven stars: 'I know your works, that you have a name that you are alive, but you are dead. Be watchful, and strengthen the things which remain, that are ready to die, for I have not found your works perfect before God. Remember therefore how you have received and heard; hold fast and repent. Therefore if you will not watch, I will come upon you as a thief, and you will not know what hour I will come upon you. You have a few names even in Sardis who have not defiled their garments; and they shall walk with Me in white, for they are worthy. He who overcomes shall be clothed in white garments, and I will not blot out his name from the Book of Life; but I will confess his name before My Father and before His angels.'"

The message of the Lord to the church in Sardis is directed toward a spiritual "deadness" that the Lord sees in those who claim to "have a name that you are alive, but you are dead." These are people who go through the motions of aligning themselves with the church and pursuing Christian disciplines, but their hearts are not truly following the leading of the Holy Spirit. Among them were those who were never genuinely born again, but who simply associated with the church and sought to have a godly reputation.

Certainly a number of people today are like the Sardinians. They attend church, they go through the motions of Christianity, but they have not truly been born again. Outwardly, they appear to be right with God, but inwardly, they have never been truly born again.

Others in Sardis were believers who had truly accepted Christ, but then had become more concerned with outward behavior than inner spiritual growth. The Lord calls them to remember the time when they received and heard the gospel and to hold fast to the living faith within their hearts and to continue to sorrow for their sinful ways. These are people who think that they have "done enough" to get into heaven, but now they are relying on their outward appearances and reputations more than they are pursuing the inner qualities and character that God desires for them.

Be watchful, and strengthen the things which remain, that are ready to die, for I have not found your works perfect before God.

—Revelation 3:2

🔊 What sort of things might God be referring to when He calls His people to "strengthen the things which remain, that are ready to die"?

🔊 How can you strengthen your understanding of eternal security by strengthening the important doctrines of Christ?

The Great White Throne Judgment

The reference made in this warning to the believers at Sardis pertains to the "Book of Life." The judgment that involves the Book of Life is not a judgment of the lost, but a judgment of believers. It is also called the Great White Throne Judgment. We read about it in Revelation 20:11–15:

Then I saw a great white throne and Him who sat on it, from whose face the earth and the heaven fled away. And there was found no place for them. And I saw the dead, small and great, standing before God, and books were opened. And another book was opened, which is the Book of Life. And the dead were judged according to their works, by the things which were written in the books. The sea gave up the dead who were in it, and Death and Hades delivered up the dead who were in them. And they were judged, each one according to his works. Then Death and Hades were cast into the lake of fire. This is the second death. And anyone not found written in the Book of Life was cast into the lake of fire.

The deeds in the Book of Life relate to the *rewards* that believers will be given. Those whose names are not in the Book of Life have already been judged before this Great White Throne Judgment takes place. Those not written in the book will be the ones who follow the "beast" that makes war against the saints. (See Rev. 13:7–8 and 17:8.) Their defeat is described in Revelation 19. At the time of the Great White Throne Judgment, those *not* in the Book of Life will receive the punishment that comes as a result of their judgment: they are cast into the lake of fire. Those whose names *are* in the Book of Life will be granted their rewards according to their works as believers.

What is at stake for the believers in Sardis are their *rewards*—not the fact that they are saved. This matter of reward is also addressed in Revelation 22:19, where we have a warning that if anyone attempts to add or take away anything from the book of Revelation, God will "take away his part from the Book of Life."

Eternal *rewards* can be won and lost. The salvation of the true believer is not what is at stake here. The main admonition to us today is this: Be *genuinely born again*. Don't accept any substitution for a true salvation—don't think that church attendance, participation in church activities, or any other outward involvement in Christian disciplines will save you. Only genuine belief in Jesus Christ as God's Son, sent to the cross to die for your sins, will result in your being born again. Only receiving Jesus Christ as your Savior will ensure that your name is written in the Book of Life.

≈ Is your name written in the Book of Life? If so, on what basis can you be sure of that?

≈ If you are unsure, take time now to ask Jesus to forgive your sins on the basis of His death and resurrection. That is the only way that a person's name can be written in the Book of Life—but once your name is written there, it can never be erased.

Other Solemn Warnings

Various other passages in the Bible—such as Psalm 69, Matthew 24, John 15, Colossians 1, and 1 John 2—are sometimes used to support the belief that it is possible for born-again believers to fall from grace. When reading passages such as these, ask yourself these questions:

🐦 *Is the writer referring to a physical death or a spiritual death?* In some of the passages used to support falling from grace, a *physical* death is being described, not a spiritual death. For example, Psalm 69 refers to physical death, not spiritual death.

🐦 *What time or era is being described by the author?* In Matthew 24–25, for example, Jesus is speaking of a time of Great Tribulation. Great deceit will fill the earth and the warning is to be watchful always for the Lord's coming, for the "elect" will be gathered to the Lord. Much of this teaching is *not* for believers.

🐦 *Is the passage related to the way that believers are to live their lives on this earth, or is it related to the salvation of the soul?* Often, you will need to see the broader context in which a selected group of verses appears. In Colossians 1:21–23, for example, we read:

> And you, who once were alienated and enemies in your mind
> by wicked works, yet now He has reconciled in the body of His
> flesh through death, to present you holy, and blameless, and
> above reproach in His sight—if indeed you continue in the
> faith, grounded and steadfast, and are not moved away from
> the hope of the gospel which you heard.

If one only reads these three verses, it may appear that a person is only going to be saved if he remains in faith and doesn't move away from the "hope of the gospel." The broader context of Colossians is this: Jesus Christ! Throughout this book, Paul lifts up Jesus as the Savior, the giver of wisdom, the principal agent of creation, and so forth. What is at stake for the Colossians is that they *continue* to place their trust in Jesus Christ and to live, pray, and speak (see Col. 4:1–6) in such a way that Jesus will have no qualms about the way they are living. Rather, He will find them to be living holy lives, blameless and above reproach. Paul warns the Colossians against the inadequacy of certain rituals and points them repeatedly toward the sufficiency of Christ and the new life that He purchased for them. At no time is salvation an issue—but rather, the quality of life that the believers are to have and the acclaim that they are to win from the Lord by following Him with faith.

Is the passage about believers or nonbelievers? John writes that some are "not of us" (1 John 2:19). That's certainly true today! Believers and nonbelievers live by different standards, have different perspectives, and are subject to different judgments. In 1 John 2, John gives a very clear delineation between believers and nonbelievers. At no time is he describing believers who have *become* nonbelievers—rather, he is describing nonbelievers as those who have never become believers. Those who are operating out of a sin nature simply cannot love or obey God's commandments as believers can.

This same difference is described by John in other terms in John 15. Those who do not abide in the true vine of Jesus Christ are "cast out as a branch" and they are subject to being thrown into the "fire" (v. 6). This refers to those who have never believed in Jesus and, therefore, have never truly abided in Him. Believers, in comparison, are pruned so that they will bear fruit.

Read Matthew 24.

*Verse 13 reads: "But he who endures to the end shall be saved." In the context of the entire chapter, what is Jesus saying here?

Read John 15.

❧ Verse 2 reads, "Every branch in Me that does not bear fruit He takes away; and every branch that bears fruit He prunes, that it may bear more fruit." In the context of the entire chapter, what is Jesus saying here?

❧ Verse 23 reads, "He who hates Me hates My Father also." Do you love Jesus or hate Him? If you answer that you love Him, what does that suggest about your eternal security?

❧ Today and Tomorrow ❧

TODAY: I UNDERSTAND THAT, ONCE MY NAME IS WRITTEN IN THE BOOK OF LIFE, IT CAN NEVER BE ERASED.

TOMORROW: I WILL SEEK THE LORD'S HELP THIS WEEK TO LIVE THE WAY A PERSON *SHOULD* LIVE WHOSE NAME IS IN THE BOOK OF LIFE.

LESSON 7

Solemn Warnings

Part 2

❧ In This Lesson ❧

LEARNING: HOW CAN JESUS HAVE DIED JUST ONCE BUT STILL PAID FOR
EVERY SIN EVER COMMITTED?

GROWING: ONCE I'M SAVED, WHY SHOULD I WORRY ABOUT GROWING IN
CHRIST?

∽

The author of Hebrews warns his readers of the perils of abandoning
the Christian faith. As we did in the previous lesson, we must take a
look at the audience to whom these warnings were made in order to
have greater insight into these passages.

The writer of Hebrews was addressing Jewish Christians. These believers had never seen Jesus personally (2:3), but they had faced intense
opposition for believing in Him (10:32–34). Through it all, however,
they had remained faithful to their newfound faith. But then some became disillusioned and drifted away (2:1). Their tendency was to re-
treat back to Judaism, which was a religion that Rome allowed.

The author of Hebrews is encouraging the Jewish Christians to *keep*
their faith in Jesus Christ. He points out Christ's superiority over the
Old Testament prophets, angels, and even Moses. He demonstrates the

preeminence of the new covenant over the old, and the book ends with an encouragement to remain faithful in the light of those who have gone before them.

It is important for us to recognize that these warnings are *not* being given to a group of people who are trying to make up their minds about Christ Jesus for the first time. The warnings are made to those who had expressed faith in Christ, who were sincere enough in their belief in Christ to suffer for Him. Furthermore, we must recognize that the question with which this group was struggling was *not* whether they should abandon God and live a sinful life. They were not grappling with whether they should readopt a sin nature, or whether this was even possible. Rather, they were grappling with what "form of religion" they were going to follow.

These Jewish Christians are unusual: they were attempting to decide if they would leave Christianity as a religion in order to adhere to a religion that demanded even more from them and allowed them less freedom! Rarely is that the case in our world. Most people opt for an easier way to please God, not a more difficult way.

> Let us hold fast the confession of our hope without wavering,
> for He who promised is faithful.

> —Hebrews 10:23

❧ What does it mean to "hold fast the confession of our hope"?

∼ What sorts of "wavering" have you experienced in your hope of salvation? How does this verse address those "waverings"?

What Hebrews Teaches

Let's consider for a moment what the book of Hebrews as a whole teaches about salvation. While we cannot do an entire survey of Hebrews in this one lesson, we can note these things about the book:

∼ No book in the New Testament other than the Gospel of John argues so conclusively in favor of a salvation that is eternally secure. The author clearly states that blood sacrifices of animals cannot accomplish what the death of Christ accomplished "once for all" (9:26–27; 10:9–14).

∼ The author clearly states that Christians are sanctified or made holy through the death of Christ *for all time* (10:5–14.)

∼ The author encourages his readers to "hold fast the confession of our hope without wavering" (10:23). Many people question whether the blood of Jesus was adequate for their salvation. What they believe is that they have to "do their part" to ensure salvation—which is adding "works" to their faith. Those who believe that they have to do something to ensure salvation will always waver in their hope because they know their own fallibility and unreliability as human beings.

Overall the writer of Hebrews presents the complete adequacy of
Christ's death as the sole means for our salvation, and he encourages believers in Christ to "hold fast" to what they have done: they received Jesus as Savior. It is highly unlikely that an author who stands
so strongly in favor of eternal security could also be an advocate for
falling from grace. The overriding message of Hebrews is that Christ
is our sufficiency; in His death is our eternal life. To add works to that
provision of Christ is to misread the true message of the author.

> And as it is appointed for men to die once, but after this
> the judgment, so Christ was offered once to bear the sins of
> many....
>
> —Hebrews 9:27–28

❧ According to this passage, why did Christ only have to die
once in order to pay for your sins?

❧ What does this suggest about your eternal security?

Warning 1:

∞ Do Not Drift or Neglect ∞

Let us turn now to the three warnings that are offered in Hebrews. The first passage is Hebrews 2:1–3:

> Therefore we must give the more earnest heed to the things we have heard, lest we drift away. For if the word spoken through angels proved steadfast, and every transgression and disobedience received a just reward, how shall we escape if we neglect so great a salvation, which at the first began to be spoken by the Lord, and was confirmed to us by those who heard Him?

The author of Hebrews seems to take the tone of a teacher who catches a student nodding off during class. "Take earnest heed! Don't drift off!" That's the intent of the phrase, "lest we drift away." The term *drifting* implies a slow, gradual process. The author of Hebrews recognized that Christians can lose interest in the things pertaining to salvation. The people that he was writing to weren't drifting from a position of being saved—they were drifting in their ideas about religion. No person comes to Christ by "drifting into" salvation, and no person can fall from grace by "drifting away" from Christ.

The author reminds them that a great deal is at stake if they "neglect" their salvation. Some people today seem to think that, after they are saved, they don't need to attend church, read their Bibles, or pray—they say to themselves and others, "Well, I'm saved. That's all that matters." Not true! "Just being saved" is only the beginning of the Christian life. There is much growing to do and many rewards to attain. If a person "neglects" his salvation and fails to move forward in his faith, he will lose a great deal, even though he does not lose his salvation.

The overall intent of the author of Hebrews in this passage is to say, "Pay attention! This is important!" It is *not* a condemnation of those who have been saved and are now in danger of being lost.

☙ What Christian disciplines—Bible reading, prayer, church attendance, etc.—do you sometimes lose interest in?

☙ What does it mean to "neglect so great a salvation"? How does this differ from "drifting away" or losing interest in living a holy life?

Warning 2:

∞ No Falling Away ∞

Hebrews 6:4–6 is another passage that is often cited as an argument for falling from grace:

> For it is impossible for those who were once enlightened, and have tasted the heavenly gift, and have become partakers of

the Holy Spirit, and have tasted the good word of God and the powers of the age to come, if they fall away, to renew them again to repentance, since they crucify again for themselves the Son of God, and put Him to an open shame.

There are some who dismiss this passage as relating only to nonbelievers, or to those who have not been genuinely born again. I believe, however, that the author makes it very clear that they were enlightened, that they tasted the heavenly gift, that they were partakers of the heavenly gift (forgiveness and receiving the Holy Spirit), and that they tasted the good word of God (which means that they knew its promises to be true).

What does it mean for these genuine believers to fall away? That is the heart of the matter. To say that they have fallen away from their position of saved believers in Christ and have thus *lost* their salvation would be a dire situation, indeed, for this passage says that a person who falls away can never regain what he has lost through future repentance. Most people who believe in falling from grace do not hold such a position—rather, they believe that it is possible to repent and fall and repent and fall, with the hope that they will die or that the Lord will come while they are in an upswing period of repentance.

I do not believe that this passage relates in the least to one's salvation, but rather that these people are being warned not to fall away from their active pursuit of the Christian faith—not to fall away into their old patterns of legalism and Jewish traditions. It is a warning against apostasy, which is the extreme falling away from the pursuit of Christ to pursue another path. It would be impossible for such a person to return to Christ through repentance because he would not even think to repent! Note that the author does not say that such a person cannot be forgiven, but that he will not be "renewed" through repentance.

In Romans 12:2 we find Paul's admonition to believers that we are *not* "conformed to this world," but that we should "be transformed by the renewing of your mind," that we might "prove what is that good and acceptable and perfect will of God." Renewal is the process of transformation from the old way that we thought, acted, and felt prior to our acceptance of Christ Jesus as our Savior, to a new way that is made possible by the Holy Spirit dwelling within us. Renewal is the result of repentance and walking into a new way of life as the Holy Spirit leads and strengthens.

Those on the verge of returning to Judaism were in danger of no longer being sensitive to the leading and guiding of the Holy Spirit. They were in danger of no longer desiring to be renewed, and thus they would no longer have any desire to repent and walk in the newness of life that Christ offered to them and the Holy Spirit made possible for them.

There are a number of Christians today who know the right thing to do but who simply choose *not* to be renewed in a specific area of their lives. They do not desire to repent and be transformed. Instead, they have chosen to live in a different way, to walk a different path. The result is that they have "fallen away" from the full potential that they could have in Christ Jesus. Repentance is so far removed from their thinking that it is like a foreign concept to them. This is the situation that the author of Hebrews warns against.

The author goes on to say that those who fall away revert to a belief in which Jesus somehow *deserved* to die for *His* misdeeds (which was the Jewish position regarding Christ), rather than Jesus *choosing* to lay down His life for *our* sins. Those who believe that Jesus *deserved* death, indeed, crucify Him again and bring shame to Him. They certainly are not likely to look to Him to lead them into a renewal of their lives.

And do not be conformed to this world, but be transformed by the renewing of your mind, that you may prove what is that good and acceptable and perfect will of God.

—Romans 12:2

🔊 What does it mean to be "conformed to this world"? How might conformity to the world cause a person to doubt his salvation?

🔊 How does a person renew his mind?

🔊 Why is it important that we renew our minds if we are to understand eternal security, according to this verse?

Warning 3:

∞ No More Offering ∞

Hebrews 10:26–31 is also often quoted in support of a falling-from-grace belief:

> For if we sin willfully after we have received the knowledge
> of the truth, there no longer remains a sacrifice for sins, but a
> certain fearful expectation of judgment, and fiery indignation
> which will devour the adversaries. Anyone who has rejected
> Moses' law dies without mercy on the testimony of two or three
> witnesses. Of how much worse punishment, do you suppose,
> will he be thought worthy who has trampled the Son of God
> underfoot, counted the blood of the covenant by which he was
> sanctified a common thing, and insulted the Spirit of grace?
> For we know Him who said, "Vengeance is Mine, I will repay,"
> says the Lord. And again, "The LORD will judge His people." It
> is a fearful thing to fall into the hands of the living God.

Reading only at the surface level, this passage seems to indicate that
those who sin "willfully" after they have been saved will no longer be
able to escape God's "fiery indignation." First, we should note that at no
time in the New Testament is a distinction made between various types,
levels, or categories of sin, including those who sin willfully and those
who sin unknowingly. Neither does the Bible ever state that Christ died
only for some sins and not others, or specifically for those sins before a
person believes versus those after. In fact, Hebrews 10:12–14 says that
He offered "one sacrifice for sins forever."

Note also that this passage begins with the word *for*, which means that
it relates to the information immediately preceding it. The verses that
lead up to this warning are words of encouragement to follow through

with a commitment to Christ in light of all that He has done for believers. "Let us draw near with a true heart in full assurance of faith," the author writes (10:22). "Let us hold fast the confession of our hope without wavering" and "let us consider one another in order to stir up love and good works" (v. 23, 24).

The logical thing to ask after such statements is, "What if we don't?" The author of Hebrews anticipates this question and answers it. The Jews to whom he is writing have lived their entire lives awaiting the Messiah, the One who would establish a new covenant so powerful that God would forget their sins forever (10:17). The author reminds these Jewish believers that their next encounter is not going to be an encounter with Christ the Savior, but with Christ the Judge. Rather than being bad news that "there no longer remains a sacrifice for sin," this word is *good* news. The fact is, the sacrifice for sin has been made! The only bad news is that God is not fond of quitters.

Again, the author is attempting to prod these believers on to godly living. The "fire" of which the author speaks is not a fire of eternal punishment—the "lake of fire" that we associate with Revelation. Rather, it is the "fiery indignation" of God's judgment. Certainly, the author states, God will judge those who turn away from Christ as Messiah. They will be chastised sharply in this life, and in eternity they will not receive any of the rewards that they could have had. They truly will suffer loss, and they should rightfully fear such a suffering, but at no time does the author state that their eternal salvation is in jeopardy. Rather, all of their rewards and their standing within the body of Christ are at stake. Truly it is "terrifying" to think of all that a person *might* have been and *might* have become and *might* have been rewarded. To the author of Hebrews, the possibility that one might stand before the judgment seat of Christ and see all his works burned to ashes would be a "much worse punishment" than even death itself (10:29).

Repeatedly, the author of Hebrews states that Christ made "one offering" for sin and that this was an eternal and never-to-be-repeated
sacrifice. If we reject Christ's salvation, we certainly are in dire danger
of being lost forever. If we accept Christ's salvation but do not continue
to trust in Him, then we are in dire danger of losing the rewards that
we might otherwise have received. That is the message of Hebrews—a
message that most certainly is a strong warning to those believers who
might be wavering in their commitment to follow Christ's example. It is
not, however, a warning that a person can lose his salvation.

> Of how much worse punishment, do you suppose, will he be
> thought worthy who has trampled the Son of God underfoot,
> counted the blood of the covenant by which he was sanctified a
> common thing, and insulted the Spirit of grace?
>
> —Hebrews 10:29

How might a Christian "trample the Son of God underfoot"?
Give practical examples. (No names, please.)

How might a Christian "insult the Spirit of Grace"? Give practical examples. (No names, please.)

❧ How are these things different from refusing to accept God's plan of salvation through Christ? How is the result different between these two types of sin?

❧ Today and Tomorrow ❧

TODAY: I UNDERSTAND THAT JESUS DIED JUST ONCE, BUT THAT I CAN TREAT THAT DEATH WITH CONTEMPT IF I DON'T OBEY.

TOMORROW: I WILL ASK THE LORD TO HELP ME GROW IN A STEADFAST DESIRE TO KEEP BECOMING MORE LIKE CHRIST.

❧ Notes and Prayer Requests: ❧

LESSON 8

A License to Sin?

LEARNING: WHERE DOES THE HOLY SPIRIT COME INTO ALL THIS?

GROWING: HOW CAN I GET RID OF MY *DESIRE* TO SIN?

Many people act as though eternal security is nothing but a license to sin. It is absolutely not! At no time in Scripture do we find God winking at sin, diminishing the importance of sin, or allowing sin to go without serious consequences. There is never a license to sin, before or after one's spiritual rebirth.

"But," someone might say, "if a person can never lose his salvation, what keeps me from living any way that I desire? I'll still make it to heaven!" In the first place, a person who is genuinely born again will not *want* to sin or live "any way that he desires." If a person still has a strong desire to sin and to live in a manner that is contrary to the will of God, then he very likely has not been genuinely born again. When a person has experienced a spiritual new birth, he is a new creature and will not *want* to sin.

Second, "just making heaven" is a poor excuse for an eternal state of being. At stake is a great loss of eternal reward, which we will cover in the next lesson.

Third, the person who pursues sin after being born again is a person who is going to experience God's chastening on this earth. Chastening can include pain, suffering, loss, and trouble. A person who accepts Christ and then refuses all prompting of the Holy Spirit to repent and be transformed is a person who is likely to experience a certain amount of "hell on earth," even though he may escape the eternal fires of hell.

In this lesson, we will take a look at both mankind's sin nature and the believer's sinful deeds, and the consequences associated with each. First, however, we'll take a brief look at the Holy Spirit's relationship to us before and after our salvation.

The Holy Spirit's Roles Related to Our Sin

Prior to our conversion, the Holy Spirit is at work in our lives to bring us to a recognition of our sin nature and to prompt us to accept Jesus as our Savior. The Holy Spirit *woos* us to Christ. The conviction that we experience prior to salvation is a conviction that is related to our sinful deeds and to the greater truth that we are sinners—we have a sin nature that must be changed. The Holy Spirit is relentless in His pursuit of us, although the unsaved person may not be aware of the Holy Spirit's work or may even deny His existence.

The person who has not been born again is subject to eternal death. That is the punishment awaiting any person who has not received Christ Jesus as Savior. This punishment is related to the sin *nature* of an unsaved person, not to specific sin *deeds*. The conviction of the Holy Spirit in the unbeliever's life is related to the Word of God. The unsaved person has a haunting "knowing" that he is estranged from God, now and forever, unless the very state of his soul is changed. The person has the knowledge that he is sinful, needs forgiveness, and that he cannot forgive himself or alter his own nature.

And when [the Holy Spirit] has come, He will convict the world
of sin, and of righteousness, and of judgment.

—John 16:8

❧ What is the Holy Spirit's role in a non-Christian's life?

❧ How does His role change after we become born again?

The Holy Spirit's work in our lives after we are born again is very different. The Holy Spirit *indwells* the one who receives Christ Jesus as Savior. No longer is He at work externally, but now internally. The Holy
Spirit illuminates the Word of God as we read it, and He uses the Word
of God to prick our conscience and to lead us to walk in right paths.
The Holy Spirit functions within us as the Spirit of Truth, showing us
God's perfect will.

When we fail to listen to the Holy Spirit and choose to walk in our own
ways rather than in God's way, the Holy Spirit chastises us. We feel uncomfortable, frustrated, and uneasy in our spirits. We know that we are
disobeying God and are not becoming the people that He wants us to

be. The nudge of the Holy Spirit is toward our *repentance*—recognizing our sinful attitudes and deeds, asking God to forgive us, and asking Him to help us to withstand temptation and follow the path that God has set before us.

The Holy Spirit leads us and enables us to act. When we fail to receive His guidance and His help, we grieve Him. We fall into error; we fail to live the way that God wants us to live. He is grieved on our behalf (see Ephesians 4:30), and He seeks to bring us back into obedience. His efforts to *correct* us and teach us are what we perceive as God's chastisement.

> ...the Spirit of truth ... will guide you into all truth; for He will not speak on His own authority, but whatever He hears He will speak; and He will tell you things to come. He will glorify Me, for He will take of what is Mine and declare it to you.
>
> —John 16:13-14

☙ According to these verses, what is the primary role of the Holy Spirit in our lives?

☙ What does it mean that He will take what is Christ's and "declare it to you"? What response does He expect from you?

Chastening vs. Punishment

The nonbeliever is subject to punishment. Punishment is irreversible; it is the consequence of an unchanged spiritual *state of being*. Punishment is, in effect, the "final sentencing." The believer, however, is subject to chastening, not punishment. Chastening is for the purpose of teaching, training, and correcting. It is always exercised for the *good* of the person—in other words, so that the person might change his ways and become more like Jesus Christ in character, attitude, and behavior. Chastening occurs in the wake of specific *sinful deeds*.

Although chastening is certainly for our good, it is nonetheless painful. Those who are born again and then choose to sin will not find that their sin goes unchastened—rather, they will discover that the longer they continue to engage in sinful attitudes and deeds, the *stronger* the chastening will become. The best thing to do when you are being chastened by God is to yield immediately, acknowledging your sin, seeking forgiveness, and asking God to help you to change your attitude or your behavior. You can greatly lessen the pain of chastening if you will respond quickly and *learn* from it. The pain will be eliminated, and you will actually be "trained" into the right way to live and experience God's peace. (See Hebrews 12:11.)

🔊 When have you experienced chastisement? How did you feel? What was the result?

You should know in your heart that as a man chastens his son, so the LORD your God chastens you. Therefore you shall keep the commandments of the LORD your God, to walk in His ways and to fear Him.

—Deuteronomy 8:5-6

▸ How is God's chastening influenced by the fact that you are His son? How should this influence your obedience?

▸ How does that relationship, as a son of God, affect your views of eternal security?

∞

Eliminating the Desire to Sin

The Holy Spirit also works within the believer to generate a *hunger and thirst* for righteousness, which might also be stated as *a lack of desire to sin*. The Holy Spirit gives us a desire to obey the commandments of God. Knowing that we are saved forever does not give the believer a freedom to sin, but rather, a freedom from all desire to sin! The believer is out of the bondage of sin, and he will not have any desire to re-enter that bondage.

John wrote, "We know that whoever is born of God does not sin; but he who has been born of God keeps himself" (1 John 5:18). John was not saying that the born-again believer will never again sin or err; rather, this verse is the conclusion to the several verses that go before it—verses that are about the "sin which leads to death." John is saying that the person who is born again no longer sins the sin that leads to death. Rather, the born-again believer has a new identity and a new desire to be so sensitive and obedient to the leading of the Holy Spirit that he will not sin. The believer will choose, by an act of the will, to "[keep] himself" away from sin and temptation. He will choose, by an act of the will, to walk in paths of righteousness.

> If we say that we have fellowship with Him, and walk in darkness, we lie and do not practice the truth. But if we walk in the light as He is in the light, we have fellowship with one another, and the blood of Jesus Christ His Son cleanses us from all sin.

> —1 John 1:6-7

☙ What does it mean to "walk in darkness"? To "walk in the light"?

☙ What does it mean to "practice the truth"? How does the Holy Spirit help us in this "practice"?

∞

What About the Unpardonable Sin?

I have talked with a number of Christians who were afraid that they might have committed "the unpardonable sin." There are hundreds of verses in the Bible that promise forgiveness of sins, but only one passage refers to an unforgivable sin. We find it in Matthew 12:31–32, where Jesus said:

> Therefore I say to you, every sin and blasphemy will be forgiven men, but the blasphemy against the Spirit will not be forgiven men. Anyone who speaks a word against the Son of Man, it will be forgiven him; but whoever speaks against the Holy Spirit, it will not be forgiven him, either in this age or in the age to come.

Let's understand the context of this verse. Jesus had healed a demon-possessed man who was blind and dumb. The multitudes began to question, "Could this be the Son of David?" The Pharisees responded to the multitudes by declaring that Jesus cast out demons by the power of Beelzebub—in other words, that Jesus was controlled by the chief of all demons. They were engaging in *blasphemy*, which is defined as "defiant irreverence."

The Pharisees had seen proof after proof that Jesus was who He claimed to be. They couldn't escape the fact that what He was doing was supernatural in nature. But instead of acknowledging that Jesus came from God, they attributed His supernatural power to Satan, rather than to the Holy Spirit. Jesus' rebuke was *directly and solely* for these false teachers in this particular setting. Jesus was saying, in effect, "If these Pharisees cannot see the truth that I do what I do by the power of the

Holy Spirit, they will never come to believe in Me and they will be lost forever. If they have so hardened their hearts against the Holy Spirit that they cannot recognize Him at work, they will not be able to believe in Me, now or in the future."

Christ is not in the world now as He was then. The Holy Spirit is still accomplishing supernatural things through His servants, yet those servants are merely representatives of the King. The circumstances of Matthew 12 make it impossible for this sin to take place today. The Bible clearly states, "Whoever calls on the name of the LORD shall be saved" (Rom. 10:13.) There is no promise related to God's forgiveness that has an "exception clause" that reads, "unless you commit the unpardonable sin."

There is no unpardonable sin today, but there is an unpardonable *state of unbelief*. There is no pardon for a person who dies in unbelief. The good news, however, is that a person does not need to remain in this state of unbelief. He can choose to believe in Jesus and receive Him as his Savior!

> Let no one say when he is tempted, "I am tempted by God";
> for God cannot be tempted by evil, nor does He Himself tempt
> anyone. But each one is tempted when he is drawn away by his
> own desires and enticed.
>
> —James 1:13-14

🕭 What is the difference between temptation and testing? What about chastening?

🕭 What is the role of the Holy Spirit in each of these things: temptation, testing, chastening?

Walking in Freedom

The promise of the Holy Spirit to every believer is this: "Listen to Me and obey My voice, and I will keep you free from sin's bondage." The Holy Spirit does not lead us into sin or into the temptation to sin. Rather, He delivers us from all evil. You can choose to walk in the freedom *from sin*—and what a great freedom that is. Never do we have a freedom *to* sin, but we do have a great promise of freedom to live *apart* from sin!

> And do not grieve the Holy Spirit of God, by whom you were sealed for the day of redemption. Let all bitterness, wrath, anger, clamor, and evil speaking be put away from you, with all malice. And be kind to one another, tenderhearted, forgiving one another, even as God in Christ forgave you.
>
> —Ephesians 4:30-32

🕭 What does it mean to "grieve the Holy Spirit of God"? What results when we do this?

 Go through the list of sins (bitterness, wrath, etc.) and godly qualities (be kind, etc.) and give examples from your own life.

 What does it mean that you were "sealed for the day of redemption" when you accepted Christ? How does this affect your views of eternal security?

Furthermore, we have had human fathers who corrected us, and we paid them respect. Shall we not much more readily be in subjection to the Father of spirits and live? For they indeed for a few days chastened us as seemed best to them, but He for our profit, that we may be partakers of His holiness. Now no chastening seems to be joyful for the present, but painful; nevertheless, afterward it yields the peaceable fruit of righteousness to those who have been trained by it.

—Hebrews 12:9-11

 How did your father chasten you when you were young? How does God's chastening compare, according to these verses?

How does a person become "trained" by chastening? What is the result of that training?

> Do not love the world or the things in the world. If anyone loves the world, the love of the Father is not in him. For all that is in the world—the lust of the flesh, the lust of the eyes, and the pride of life—is not of the Father but is of the world.
>
> —1 John 2:15-16

Define "lust of the flesh," "lust of the eyes," and "pride of life," giving practical examples of each.

Is your life characterized by any of these traits? How will you work this week at strengthening those areas?

❦ Today and Tomorrow ❧

TODAY: THE HOLY SPIRIT CHASTENS ME AND STRENGTHENS ME, GRADU-
ALLY REMOVING MY DESIRE TO SIN.

TOMORROW: I WILL ASK THE LORD TO SHOW ME AREAS WHERE I NEED TO
FOLLOW THE HOLY SPIRIT'S LEADING MORE.

❦ Notes and Prayer Requests: ❧

LESSON 9

Eternal Rewards

─── ❧ **In This Lesson** ❧ ───

LEARNING: WHAT REWARDS DO CHRISTIANS RECEIVE IN HEAVEN?

GROWING: HOW CAN I ENSURE THAT I RECEIVE MY SHARE OF ETERNAL REWARDS?

❧

Eternal security is not equal to eternal rewards. Rewards are related to our *works* as believers—what we do for the Lord, and the works that we allow the Lord to do in us. "Works," from a Bible perspective, include:

❧ Attitudes   ❧ Motives   ❧ Conduct   ❧ Service

On these two points we must be very clear:

1. Works can never earn salvation. We are saved solely by our faith in the Lord Jesus Christ as God's Son.

2. All of the believer's works are evaluated by the Lord. Works are related to the rewards that each believer will receive from the Lord. Some rewards may be received in this life, but the vast majority of our rewards are reserved for us in eternity.

Many Christians just want to get into heaven. They think that they will be satisfied if they can just get through the pearly gates. That is not at all the attitude that God wants us to have. Our goal as Christians should be to live in a way that will be highly rewarded by the Lord. It should be the desire of every believer to hear the Lord say one day, "Well done, thou good and faithful servant."

All Works Are Evaluated

The Scriptures declare repeatedly that all of our works are evaluated after salvation. We each will be fully accountable for our lives and how we spent our time, talents, and resources. There is no such thing as "neutrality" when it comes to our attitudes, motives, deeds, and behaviors after we are saved. Every deed, and every lack of deed, is subject to judgment. As we read in Colossians 3:23–25, we will receive "payment" for all that we do:

> And whatever you do, do it heartily, as to the Lord and not to men, knowing that from the Lord you will receive the reward of the inheritance; for you serve the Lord Christ. But he who does wrong will be repaid for what he has done, and there is no partiality.

∞ Rewards and Repayments ∞

In the first few chapters of Revelation, we find a sharp distinction between "rewards" for service to the Lord and "repayment" for wrongs. Here are just a few of these contrasts:

> "Nevertheless I have this against you, that you have left your first love. Remember therefore from where you have fallen; repent and do the first works, or else I will come to you quickly

and remove your lampstand from its place—unless you repent. ... To him who overcomes I will give to eat from the tree of life, which is in the midst of the Paradise of God" (Revelation 2:4–5, 7).

"I have a few things against you, because you have there those who hold the doctrine of Balaam, who taught Balak to put a stumbling block before the children of Israel, to eat things sacrificed to idols, and to commit sexual immorality.... Repent, or else I will come to you quickly and will fight against them with the sword of My mouth.... To him who overcomes I will give some of the hidden manna to eat. And I will give him a white stone, and on the stone a new name written which no one knows except him who receives it" (Revelation 2:14, 16–17).

"I know your works, love, service, faith, and your patience; and as for your works, the last are more than the first. Nevertheless I have a few things against you, because you allow that woman Jezebel, who calls herself a prophetess, to teach and seduce My servants to commit sexual immorality and eat things sacrificed to idols. And I gave her time to repent of her sexual immorality, and she did not repent. Indeed I will cast her into a sickbed, and those who commit adultery with her into great tribulation, unless they repent of their deeds. I will kill her children with death, and all the churches shall know that I am He who searches the minds and hearts. And I will give to each one of you according to your works. . . . He who overcomes, and keeps My works until the end, to him I will give power over the nations" (Revelation 2:19–23, 26).

Surely there can be no doubt that God's "rewards" are generous and life-giving and His "repayments" are to be avoided!

Do not be deceived, God is not mocked; for whatever a man sows, that he will also reap. For he who sows to his flesh will of the flesh reap corruption, but he who sows to the Spirit will of the Spirit reap everlasting life. And let us not grow weary while doing good, for in due season we shall reap if we do not lose heart. Therefore, as we have opportunity, let us do good to all, especially to those who are of the household of faith.

—Galatians 6:7-10

What does it mean to "sow to the flesh"? To "sow to the Spirit"? Give practical examples of each.

In what ways might a person "grow weary while doing good"? What can we do to avoid that?

∞ No Tolerance for the "Lukewarm" ∞

We read these sobering words in Revelation 3:15–16:

> I know your works, that you are neither cold nor hot. I could wish you were cold or hot. So then, because you are lukewarm, and neither cold nor hot, I will vomit you out of My mouth.

Furthermore, the Lord wants us to seek what *He* defines as spiritual riches and genuine spiritual wealth. He wants us to pursue all that He has for us, to never be satisfied with our current level of spiritual maturity. No part of us is yet fully like Jesus Christ. There is always more of His character that we must aspire to attain. For example:

∞ To be more and more refined and made pure in spirit.

∞ To have greater and greater insight into God's Word and His purpose for our lives.

∞ To be zealous for the things of the Lord.

∞ To allow the Lord entrance into every area of our lives, every minute of our lives, and to develop an intimate relationship with Him.

We never "arrive" as Christians. Our desire must be to pursue the fullness of Christ Jesus *intensely* and with great *focus*.

∞

Because you say, 'I am rich, have become wealthy, and have
need of nothing'—and do not know that you are wretched, mis-
erable, poor, blind, and naked—I counsel you to buy from Me
gold refined in the fire, that you may be rich; and white garments, that you may be clothed, that the shame of your naked-
ness may not be revealed; and anoint your eyes with eye salve,
that you may see. As many as I love, I rebuke and chasten.
Therefore be zealous and repent. Behold, I stand at the door
and knock. If anyone hears My voice and opens the door, I will
come in to him and dine with him, and he with Me.

—Revelation 3:17-20

❧ What does it mean to be "zealous"? What does zeal for Christ
look like in real life?

❧ What "gold" do we "buy" from God? What "white garments"?
How do we "buy" them?

Choosing the Best Building Materials

The apostle Paul wrote about the works of believers in Corinthians 3:10–15:

> According to the grace of God which was given to me, as a wise master builder I have laid the foundation, and another builds on it. But let each one take heed how he builds on it. For no other foundation can anyone lay than that which is laid, which is Jesus Christ. Now if anyone builds on this foundation with gold, silver, precious stones, wood, hay, straw, each one's work will become clear; for the Day will declare it, because it will be revealed by fire; and the fire will test each one's work, of what sort it is. . . . If anyone's work is burned, he will suffer loss; but he himself will be saved, yet so as through fire.

Consider two things about this passage:

First, Paul characterizes our works as being either combustible or fireproof. When our works are evaluated in eternity, some of them are going to be reduced to a pile of ashes. We will have invested our time, talents, and resources into things that simply have no lasting value. Other works will be ones that remain and become purer and brighter when tested by fire. We are called to set the things of God as our first priority—seeking His kingdom on a daily, even hourly basis is the most important priority that we can have (see Matthew 6:10). If we make the Lord's will our will, all other things fall into place. When we put our thoughts, words, and deeds into the context of eternity, we generally have a clearer picture of what is truly important and what has lasting value. Only those things that are done by and for Christ Jesus will last forever.

Second, Paul speaks of building on a foundation—with wood, hay, and stubble, or with gold, silver, and precious stones. What is this foundation on which we are building? Paul states, "We are God's fellow workers; you are God's field, you are God's building" (1 Corinthians 3:9). The building materials that Paul describes are ones used to build up other people. Paul is describing the character of our witness—the lasting value of our service or ministry to others. Can anything be of more value to a sinner than a person sharing the gospel of Jesus Christ with him? Can anything be of more help to a hurting person than to experience a generous outpouring of God's love? We must make it our number one intent to share all that we have of Christ with as many as possible in any given day of our lives. In this way, we extend the gospel of Christ Jesus.

Who has built upon the foundation of Christ in your life, in a way that is eternally valuable? Whose life have you built up "with gold, silver, and precious stones"?

Read Romans 12. What practical ways does Paul suggest for building up others "with gold, silver, and precious stones"?

∞ Not All Positions in Eternity are Equal ∞

The saints in heaven are not all going to have the same roles or oc-
cupy the same positions of authority. Some who are in great positions
of power and authority here on earth, for example, will not have any
power or authority in heaven. Others who seem to be the least here on
earth will be among those who have authority and power in heaven.
God will evaluate the intent, faithfulness, and purity of each person's
heart, and on that basis He will establish the "rulership" of heaven.
(See Matthew 19:30.)

We also read in the Scriptures about various "crowns" that will be given
to believers. Crowns are signs of authority. These crowns are given to
believers as part of their eternal reward. (See Revelation 4:4, 10).

∞ Not the Same Degree of Joy ∞

Furthermore, not all believers in heaven will be able to enjoy heaven to
the same degree. We all take comfort from these words in Revelation
21:3–4:

> God Himself will be with them and be their God. And God will
> wipe away every tear from their eyes; there shall be no more
> death, nor sorrow, nor crying. There shall be no more pain, for
> the former things have passed away.

Life in heaven will bear these characteristics for *all*, but the Scriptures
also speak of a growing maturity of faith that will produce rewards. In
2 Corinthians 3:18 we read:

> But we all, with unveiled face, beholding as in a mirror the
> glory of the Lord, are being transformed into the same image
> from glory to glory, just as by the Spirit of the Lord.

Those who allow the Holy Spirit to transform their lives and bring about spiritual maturity are going to be able to experience more of the glory of the Lord in eternity. They are going to have a greater capacity for joy, a greater capacity for praise, a deeper and richer understanding of God, and a closer intimacy with the Father.

> And everyone who has left houses or brothers or sisters or father or mother or wife or children or lands, for My name's sake, shall receive a hundredfold, and inherit eternal life. But many who are first will be last, and the last first.
>
> —Matthew 19:29-30

🔊 Who do you know that might be considered among the "last" here on earth, but who is likely to be among the "first" in heaven? What is it about that person's life that makes you say this?

On What Basis are We Judged?

Scriptures make it clear that we are not going to be compared to *others* when our works are judged. Rather, what we do and who we are will be judged against our God-given potential and God's plan for our lives. We have all been given very specific talents, opportunities, privileges, and a measure of time. What we *do* with God's gifts to us, and what we allow God to do in us and through us, are what will be judged.

As you read the passage of Scripture that follows, note that we are going to be judged on:

- The basis of what we do to others.

- The degree to which we know and prepare ourselves to do the will of our Master.

- How much has been given to us or entrusted to us.

And the Lord said, "Who then is that faithful and wise steward, whom his master will make ruler over his household, to give them their portion of food in due season? Blessed is that servant whom his master will find so doing when he comes. Truly, I say to you that he will make him ruler over all that he has. But if that servant says in his heart, 'My master is delaying his coming,' and begins to beat the male and female servants, and to eat and drink and be drunk, the master of that servant will come on a day when he is not looking for him, and at an hour when he is not aware, and will cut him in two and appoint him his portion with the unbelievers. And that servant who knew his master's will, and did not prepare himself or do according to his will, shall be beaten with many stripes. But he who did not know, yet committed things deserving of stripes, shall be beaten with few. For everyone to whom much is given, from him much will be required; and to whom much has been committed, of him they will ask the more.

—Luke 12:42-48

≈ What have you been given in your life? How well are you using those gifts in service to Christ?

≈ If Jesus returns tonight, will you be judged a "wise steward" or a "foolish steward"?

> ...He who judges me is the Lord. Therefore judge nothing before the time, until the Lord comes, who will both bring to light the hidden things of darkness and reveal the counsels of the hearts. Then each one's praise will come from God.
>
> —1 Corinthians 4:4-5

≈ What does it mean that the Lord will "bring to light the hidden things of darkness"? That He will "reveal the counsels of the hearts"?

❧ If you were called before God today, what "hidden things of darkness" would He reveal in your life? How would the "counsels of your heart" be judged?

> Your kingdom come. Your will be done On earth as it is in heaven.

> —Matthew 6:10

❧ Describe how God's will is "done" in heaven. How would things be different if His will were done that way on earth today?

❧ How can you improve how God's will is accomplished in your life this week?

╾───── ∾ **Today and Tomorrow** ∾ ─────╼

TODAY: MY ETERNAL REWARDS WILL BE BASED UPON HOW FAITHFUL I AM
IN SERVICE TO CHRIST—TODAY AND TOMORROW.

TOMORROW: I WILL ASK THE LORD TO SHOW ME WAYS IN WHICH I CAN
SERVE HIM MORE FULLY THIS WEEK.

∾

∾ Notes and Prayer Requests: ∾

Living in the Assurance of Eternal Security

❧ In This Lesson ❧

LEARNING: WHAT THINGS ARE ROBBING ME OF MY PEACE AND JOY?

GROWING: HOW CAN I OVERCOME MY DOUBTS AND FEARS?

∞

I have never met a Christian who has lost his salvation. However, I have met plenty who have lost their *assurance.* Our *security* rests in the hands of an unconditionally loving heavenly Father who gave His best, His only begotten Son, Jesus Christ, to ensure our fellowship with Him forever. Our *assurance* rests in understanding and accepting His provision and the truth that our salvation is eternally secure.

There are three things that can rob us of our assurance. We must be on guard against them at all times:

1. Guilt, which arises when we do not seek forgiveness for our sins

2. Doubt that produces fear

3. Pride and feelings of self-sufficiency

Guilt Can Rob Us of Assurance

Guilt is the natural response to sin. Most people are trained from an early age to have an understanding between right and wrong. When we know that we have done wrong, we *expect* a disciplinary response, and until we receive it, we live in anticipation of it. We know that we deserve chastening or punishment. The anticipation of punishment and chastening is guilt. The problem is that believers have either ascribed the wrong "punishment" to their sins, or they have not sought and received the forgiveness that God makes available to them.

When we sin as believers, we must go immediately to our heavenly Father and ask His forgiveness. We must go with the assurance that when we ask, He forgives. We then must move forward in our lives, forgiving ourselves even as God has forgiven us. We are wise to make amends to those that we have hurt by our sin, but we must not continue to harbor guilt for something that God has forgiven.

Then, we must take the additional step of asking the Holy Spirit to help us *not* to engage in that sin again. We must be sensitive to His leading us *away* from temptation. We must ask for His help to withstand temptation when it arises. (See Matthew 6:13.)

I have encountered a number of people who think that they have sinned too many times since their salvation for God to continue to extend His mercy and forgiveness to them. They say, in effect, "I've worn out God's patience. Surely He can't continue to forgive me since I've sinned so many times, or committed such a great sin." The fact is, God's mercy and forgiveness cannot be measured in human terms; God's capacity to forgive is as infinite as God.

There is a "cure" for sin and guilt: God's forgiveness! Turn to the Lord with your guilt and receive His forgiveness, regardless of the quantity or type of your sins. Do not let guilt rob you of your assurance that you are saved and eternally secure in your relationship with your loving heavenly Father.

> If we confess our sins, He is faithful and just to forgive us our sins and to cleanse us from all unrighteousness.
>
> —1 John 1:9

✎ What is required of a Christian if he is to be forgiven of a sin?

✎ According to this verse, how does God go *beyond* merely forgiving us of sin?

Doubt-Based Fear Can Rob Us of Assurance

Fear of God's punishments can cause paralysis in a believer, even to the point where the person no longer feels free to serve others or to minister in ways that the Holy Spirit desires. Such a gripping fear is a work of Satan. It is rooted in Satan's lies about God, which cause the person to doubt God's love and mercy.

The basic lie that Satan feeds to a believer is this: "God is a hard task-master; He demands absolute perfection and obedience. He punishes severely all those who disobey Him." The devil will never tell a person how much God loves him, or how God has provided the means for a person to have his sin nature transformed through believing in Jesus Christ as his Savior.

What motivated God to send Jesus to die on the cross in your place? Love. Jesus said it plainly, "For God *so loved the world...*" (John 3:16, italics added). The sole motivation for God's mercy and kindness is love—a love of such magnitude that all human illustrations fall short, a love that is unconditional at its core with no hidden agendas and no fine print. God's love is such that He accepts us just the way we are—but He refuses to leave us there.

Our expression of faith in Jesus places us into an unconditional, loving relationship with our heavenly Father. His offer of salvation is made to all people everywhere. Some choose to accept it by faith, others will reject it. But the offer remains. Such is the nature of God's love.

Certainly there are those who will abuse God's mercy and forgiveness. But God's love is so pure that He will not go back on His word even to those who abuse their relationship with Him. He remains faithful to the faithless. Nothing can separate us from God's love. No one can snatch us from His hand. Where sin abounds, grace *super*-abounds. Anything less would be less than unconditional.

Any time that you begin to doubt God's love for you, immerse yourself again in the Scriptures that speak of God's love, His forgiveness, and His free offer of salvation and everlasting life. Ask the Lord to help you to believe even more fully that He loves you. As one person cried out to Jesus, "Lord, I believe; help my unbelief!" (Mark 9:24) Do not let a doubt-induced fear paralyze you and keep you from experiencing full assurance of your salvation and God's love for you.

❄ When have you felt that God's love is too good to be true? Have you doubted God's love for you?

❄ Have you called out to God, saying, "Lord, help my unbelief"?

Some Christians begin to doubt God's love when they sin and experience God's chastening. They associate the pain and sorrow that they feel with judgment and anger, rather than with love. The Lord chastens us out of His love, but what we *feel* when we are being chastened may not be feelings that we associate with love. A young child who is being spanked is likely *not* to think of his parent's love while the spanking is being administered, although the parent's love for the child never changes. It is love that motivates the parent to discipline his child so that the child will experience a better future. What we *feel* is never a good gauge for what is *truth*. God loves us and His love toward us does not diminish, regardless of the chastening that we may receive.

> Though He causes grief, Yet He will show compassion according to the multitude of His mercies. For He does not afflict willingly, nor grieve the children of men.

> —Lamentations 3:32-33

✎ What do these verses suggest about God's discipline in our lives?

✎ What does this suggest about your eternal security?

Pride Can Rob Us of Assurance

The third great enemy of our assurance of salvation is our own pride. It is an expression of pride to believe that *we* must contribute something to our own salvation—that we can do something to further the work of Jesus on the cross. So many Christians try to compensate for their own sins. In the process, they eventually discover that they cannot do even those things that they should do! A spirit of striving sets in, and soon the person loses the joy of the Lord and becomes discouraged. A person who is striving to do the "right things" in order to be pleasing to God and to ensure his own salvation is a person who is going to be far less fruitful in his life. He will not be fully yielded to the Holy Spirit, so that the Holy Spirit might produce the fruit of His own character in his life. (See Galations 5:22, 25.) A spirit of striving produces tension, anxiety, and frustration.

The cure for pride, of course, is to bow before God in humility and say simply, "I surrender all. I give You all that I am. I am Yours. Do with me as You will." A person who truly surrenders all to the Lord will soon discover that he *receives* all of the Lord in return!

> ...Seek those things which are above, where Christ is, sitting at the right hand of God. Set your mind on things above, not on things on the earth. For you died, and your life is hidden with Christ in God.

> —Colossians 3:1-3

❧ What does it mean that "your life is hidden with Christ in God"? What does this suggest about eternal security?

❧ If you are eternally secure—if you are absolutely assured of spending eternity with God—then why should you be "setting your mind on things above" while on earth?

Remaining Worthy?

Some Christians regard their good works as a means of remaining "worthy" of God's love and salvation. Friend, if that is your position today, I must tell you: You can *never* be worthy of God's ongoing salvation of your soul on the basis of your works. The fact is, nothing you ever did or thought to do made you "good" enough to deserve the death of Jesus Christ on the cross. Christ died for you while you were a sinner. If you had been capable of achieving perfection on your own, He would have had no reason to shed His blood for you. However, you are *not* capable of ever achieving perfection on your own or of transforming your own sin nature into a nature of righteousness before God. You were not worthy of your salvation, but praise God, Jesus Christ was worthy of winning that salvation for you! He took your place and He purchased for you a salvation that He then offered to you freely.

Now, as a believer in Christ Jesus, the Lord declares you worthy of eternal life. You are worthy of the Holy Spirit. You are now worthy because Jesus declares you to be worthy! Worthiness from God's perspective is *never* based upon what you have done, do, or will do. Worthiness is based solely on who Jesus is, what He has done, and what He declares on your behalf.

You can neither obtain nor ensure your salvation with good works; you can only receive God's salvation with a humble heart and submit your life to Him daily so that you might truly walk in His ways to the glory of His name.

"GOD RESISTS THE PROUD, BUT GIVES GRACE TO THE HUMBLE." Therefore submit to God....

—James 4:6-7

❧ In what way does God "resist the proud"? What kind of pride is James speaking of here?

❧ In practical terms, how can you humble yourself before God this week?

Choosing What You Will Believe

You have a choice to make. You can choose to receive forgiveness and live in freedom from guilt. You can choose to receive God's love and live in freedom from a doubt-induced fear. You can choose to humble yourself and trust God completely with your life. In making these choices, you *will* know with total *assurance* that your salvation is eternally secure.

On the other hand, you can choose to hold on to your guilt, nurse your doubts about God's love, and continue to strive to "earn" your salvation. In making these choices, you will experience a great deal of frustration, discouragement, sorrow, and a lack of enthusiasm for the things of

God. Furthermore, you will not have the "blessed assurance" that God desires for you. Your salvation may be eternally secure, but you will have none of the joy that comes in believing that you are secure!

∞ The Impact on Your Witness ∞

The assurance that you have about your salvation directly affects your witness for Jesus Christ. Those who *know* that they are eternally secure are those who have a great deal of boldness and freedom to share the gospel with others. Their lives attract sinners to Christ. Those who question their salvation and live without assurance are reluctant and ineffective in their witness. What you believe about Christ's sacrifice will directly affect the degree to which you confess Christ to others.

Choose to place your trust squarely in God's love, the definitive sacrificial work of Jesus Christ on the cross, and in God's plan for your eternal life. The choice to trust is just that—a *choice* that God calls you to make.

Trust in the LORD with all your heart, and lean not on your own understanding; In all your ways acknowledge Him, and He shall direct your paths. Do not be wise in your own eyes; Fear the LORD and depart from evil. It will be health to your flesh, and strength to your bones.

—Proverbs 3:5-8

In what ways does fearing the Lord and departing from evil bring health and strength to a believer? How might the opposite bring weakness and poor health?

🔊 What does it mean to "lean on your own understanding"? How can this lead to doubts about your eternal security?

> The Lord is not slack concerning His promise, as some count slackness, but is longsuffering toward us, not willing that any should perish but that all should come to repentance.
>
> —2 Peter 3:9

🔊 The "promise" which Peter refers to is the promise that Jesus will return to earth. What should be the Christian's focus, according to this verse?

> And do not lead us into temptation, But deliver us from the evil one. For Yours is the kingdom and the power and the glory forever. Amen.
>
> —Matthew 6:13

🔊 How has God promised to "deliver us" from temptation?

🐾 If God is faithful to deliver you "from the evil one," what does that suggest about your eternal security?

As many as I love, I rebuke and chasten. Therefore be zealous and repent.

—Revelation 3:19

🐾 When have you experienced the Lord's chastening in the past? Are you experiencing it now?

🐾 How can an understanding of this verse help you to profit from times of chastening?

Greater love has no one than this, than to lay down one's life for his friends. You are My friends if you do whatever I command you.

—John 15:13-14

❦ In what way is Jesus' friendship conditional, according to these verses?

❦ On a scale of 1 to 10, how good a "friend" have you been recently?

❦ Today and Tomorrow ❦

TODAY: FEAR AND PRIDE AND UNCONFESSED SIN WILL ROB ME OF MY PEACE CONCERNING ETERNAL SECURITY.

TOMORROW: I WILL ASK THE LORD TO SHOW ME AREAS IN MY LIFE THAT ARE INTERFERING WITH HIS WORK OF HOLINESS IN MY LIFE.

C

CPSIA information can be obtained
at www.ICGtesting.com
Printed in the USA
LVHW041218251121
704442LV00005B/58